FO[illegible]EN
Forever

FORGIVEN Forever

Living in the death of Jesus

RORY SHINER

matthiasmedia
SYDNEY • YOUNGSTOWN

Forgiven Forever

Matthias Media
(St Matthias Press Ltd ACN 067 558 365)
Email: info@matthiasmedia.com.au
Internet: www.matthiasmedia.com.au
Please visit our website for current postal and telephone contact information.

Matthias Media (USA)
Email: sales@matthiasmedia.com
Internet: www.matthiasmedia.com
Please visit our website for current postal and telephone contact information.

ISBN 978 1 922980 02 1

Cover design by Nicole Zhang.
Grid and series concept design by Annesa Fung.
Typesetting by Lankshear Design.
Discussion guide by Geoff Robson.

For my parents, Jim and Alison, who were the first
to teach me why Jesus died.

And for Philippa, my sister, who lives it out.

CONTENTS

INTRODUCTION
Why did Jesus of Nazareth die?

What sort of question are we asking?

This book is given over to answering the question of why Jesus of Nazareth died. It's an odd question to ask in some ways. What exactly are we asking?

It could, of course, be a *medical* question. History tells us that Jesus died by crucifixion, and a coronial inquest might want to go into exactly how crucifixion brings about someone's demise. What would his death certificate have said? Was exposure, or asphyxiation, or heart failure the actual cause? Jesus did, after all, die with unusual speed. A death by crucifixion often took days; for Jesus it was a mere six hours. There's something worth exploring.

Historians, on the other hand, are interested in the *historical* causes of Jesus' death. A historian might ask whether the claim that Jesus died by crucifixion is historically plausible. The French atheist Michel Onfray claimed several years ago that the Romans didn't crucify Jews at this period in history, and therefore the claim that Jesus died by crucifixion was historically suspect. Onfray's claim is a little perplexing, given the preponderance of evidence for first-century Roman executions of Jews. Still, it is a claim that could be posed and answered in good faith by historical method.

Political scientists might be interested in the *political* causes. On which charges, and under whose authority, and through the action of which political actors, was Jesus crucified? What aspects of the Roman judicial system were in play? Was it, legally speaking, unjust? Whose interests were advanced or impeded by his death?

These are all valid questions, and Christian theology is not easily partitioned off from politics, history, or even medical science. But the primary purpose of this book is to address the question *theologically*. Theology is the study of God and his ways. And in this book, we're primarily asking: what was God doing in the death of Jesus?

But even with this specific focus, we have plenty to work with.

Forgiveness of sins?

Why did Jesus die? The instinctive Christian answer is, of course, that Jesus died to forgive our sins. Isn't that it, really?

The first thing to say is, "Yes! That's it!" Jesus died so

that our sins could be forgiven. Amen! Even as I write I am humming in my head the words of the hymn:

> Jesus paid it all,
> All to him I owe;
> Sin had left a crimson stain,
> He washed it white as snow.[1]

I'm tearing up just a little bit at the very thought.

But even if we were to spend all our time on the cross as the means of the forgiveness of sins, we'd still have some work to do, and many questions to answer.

Why does forgiveness require the death of Jesus in the first place? Couldn't God just forgive? If that's what God requires of us, then why doesn't he do the same himself? Why does *Jesus'* death bring the forgiveness of sins? Would the death of any perfect person have achieved the same result? Do we live in a universe where there is some deep magic associated with such a death? What if Jesus had died as a baby, or in old age, or through a long battle with cancer? Would our sins have been forgiven then? If not, why not?

Even if this entire book were given over to Jesus' death for the forgiveness of sins, that would be enough to keep us occupied.

But according to the Bible, the death of Jesus does more (not less) than that. The death of Jesus achieves a bewildering host of outcomes. It defeats Satan, it overthrows the "rulers" and "authorities" in the heavenly

1 EM Hall, 'Jesus Paid it All' [hymn], 1865.

realms (Eph 6:12), and it reconciles Jew and Gentile. The death of Jesus affects the way we share meals and visit restaurants, love strangers and plant churches, read the Old Testament and worship God. It should shape everything from our national politics to our life and home. The cross changes everything.

The contested meaning of the cross

When it first happened, Jesus' crucifixion wasn't an event in search of meaning. Christians didn't have to pour meaning into a vacuum. It already meant something. It meant something to the Romans. It meant something to the Jews. The challenge for the early Christians was to persuade the world not that it meant *something at all*, but that it meant something *else*.

The Romans, you see, weren't just executing people in the only way they knew how. For Roman crucifixions, 'cruel and unusual' was the whole point. It was both cruel and unusual by design. For this reason, it was reserved for insurrectionists, slaves and rebels.

One of the features of crucifixion, according to first-century historian Josephus, is that the executioners could contort the body however they wanted: arms up or arms down; right way up or upside down; weird clothes or nakedness. Whatever. You were in control—the body of the condemned was your toy to have fun with. This person wasn't just being killed; they were being shamed.

The death was slow. The sheer height of the victim

made the death public and easily observed. The opportunities for humiliation were legion. For Rome, crucifixion meant, "This is a non-person. This is what comes of people who dare take us on. Accord him no dignity. Feel free to laugh."

For the Jewish people, with imaginations steeped in Scripture, the cross had another meaning. The Bible gave a very specific interpretation of the death of anyone who died in such a manner: "anyone who is hung on a pole is under God's curse" (Deut 21:23). For Bible-soaked Jews, death on a cross meant "cursed by God". Expressed as a syllogism, we could put it this way:

> Premise one: Anyone hung on a pole is cursed by God.
> Premise two: Jesus was hung on a pole.
> Conclusion: Jesus was cursed by God.

Any claim that Jesus was in fact David's true son and the Blessed One of God faced the seemingly insurmountable challenge of the manner of his death.

You see, if Jesus died at 3 pm on Friday April 33 AD, already by 3:01 pm it *meant* something.[2] For the Romans,

2 In using this date, I'm following the work of Andreas J Köstenberger and Justin Taylor (with Alexander Stewart) in their book *The Final Days of Jesus: The most important week of the most important person who ever lived* (Crossway, 2014). As they acknowledge, the date of Jesus' death is disputed: many Christian historians favour a date in 30 AD, while others opt for 33 AD. But while it's an interesting historical debate—and a useful reminder that the crucifixion is a real event in real history—our preferred date is unimportant.

it meant ‘failure’, ‘non-person’, ‘usurper’, ‘shamed’. For the Jews, it meant “cursed”—and, by biblical precedent, ‘not our true king’. Christian sense-making had to contend with the sense others had already made. The early Christians had their work cut out for them. The New Testament is our record of how they faced this enormous communicative challenge. Getting from “death by crucifixion” to “God has displayed his power and wisdom in the death of a man on a cross” was not an easy step to make. But the whole coherence and power of the Christian gospel relies on making precisely that move.

We are certainly interested in theological questions about the death of Jesus. But truth be told, my endgame is not academic, but (like all good theology) practical. The pulsing heart behind this book is not a conviction that the cross is under-taught, but rather that it is under-lived. I cannot think of a single passage in the New Testament that was written simply to teach the doctrine of the cross in the abstract. Every single New Testament mention of the cross is first and foremost an urgent appeal to live the cross. The doctrine, rich though it is, is a means to that end.

Put the other way around, it’s hard to think of many practical problems addressed in the New Testament for which the cross isn’t part of the solution. Attitudes toward government, marriage, dining habits, ethnic tensions, courtship dramas, church growth strategies, spiritual warfare, parenting, overcoming tyranny, industrial relations—all of these are topics about which New Testament authors think to themselves, "Do you know what will fix that? A better understanding of the cross."

The cross is a vast ocean of spiritual power and liveable truth. Too often we are content to play on that ocean's shore. My prayer for you as you read this book is that you'll be at least encouraged to come in up to your knees. Then, once you've gone that far, you'll feel how fresh the water is, and you'll just keep swimming.

Chapter 1

THE JESUS MEAL

Time: Thursday 2 April, 33 AD, evening
Place: Upper Room, Jerusalem

Jesus on the death of Jesus

> While they were eating, Jesus took bread, and when he had given thanks, he broke it and gave it to his disciples, saying, "Take and eat; this is my body." (Matt 26:26)

Ty Treadwell and Michelle Vernon's book *Last Suppers* is a record of final meals chosen by inmates on death row.[3] Victor Feguer (hanged 1963) chose for his last meal a single olive. John Wayne Gacy (executed 1994)

3 T Treadwell and M Vernon, *Last Suppers: Famous final meals from death row,* CreateSpace Independent Publishing Platform, 2011.

went for a bucket of Original Recipe KFC, deep-fried prawns, chips, and a punnet of strawberries. Ronnie Lee Gardner (executed 2010) ordered steak, lobster tail, apple pie and ice cream, which he ate while watching the extended edition of *The Lord of the Rings*.

The book is macabre but fascinating. The whole tradition of allowing the condemned to choose their last meal is so strange, but it reflects something profound: our meals can *mean* something. For we humans, eating is more than refuelling. Our meals can be theatres by which we assert identity, culture and value. A birthday cake, the first meal of a married couple, your last meal—these meals carry meaning. They tell us something about who we think we are, and what we think matters.

The task of understanding the cross as the action of God did not first fall to the early Christian preachers, but to Jesus himself. Jesus preached the cross. He spoke many times about his death. Some of his most concentrated teaching about the cross happened at and through a meal. It is to that meal we now turn.

The meaning of the Passover

For his last meal, Jesus chose the Passover. Why? At the time of Jesus, the Jewish people had several major festivals—harvest festivals, festivals celebrating the giving of the law, and festivals celebrating the rededication of the temple. They had a festival specifically focused on the forgiveness of sins, Yom Kippur (the Day of Atonement).

If Jesus wanted to time his death for a festival, he had a rich suite of options. He chose the Passover, and we should take that seriously: he's telling us something.

Passover was a politically charged moment for the Jewish people, and it's not hard to see why. If you were a Jew, you were celebrating the fact that you were once slaves, but now you were free. You once laboured under an oppressive foreign power in Egypt, but God defeated the Egyptians and their gods. He brought judgement on the nation that oppressed you, but he passed you over so that you were free to live under God's rule and to worship him.

How could you possibly celebrate all of that without also reflecting on your current circumstances of being under Roman occupation? Almost everything this meal says you are, you're not. It says you're free, but you're not. It says you've escaped the rule of foreign powers, but you haven't. It says your sins are forgiven, but are they? It says death has passed you by, but has it? Passover in the first century went from being a celebration of who you are to a battle cry for who you want to be. And as all those hopes were rekindled, the city of Jerusalem was like a tinderbox. The occupying forces were on high alert. The atmosphere would have been thick with a heady mixture of hope and longing. When would God bring his kingdom? And should we be doing something to nudge things along?

This is the context of Jesus' last supper. This is the meal that he chose to provide the grid by which we could understand his death.

Jesus and the new meaning of the Passover

It's worth stating the blindingly obvious: the last supper was a meal, not a church service. And Jesus didn't talk about a meal; he participated in one. It was a meal familiar to all of his disciples since childhood, in much the same way that people today might be familiar with American Thanksgiving, Chinese Reunion Dinner or British Christmas. It's that sort of meal. And in the middle of it, Jesus takes things in a surprising direction. He started to make this traditional, meaning-laden meal all about himself.

To do this, Jesus used the bread and the wine. In the context of a Passover meal, these were not his only options. On the table before him there would likely have been bitter herbs (perhaps representing the bitterness of slavery), maybe eggs, and certainly lamb—the meal's *pièce de résistance*, recalling the lambs whose blood was painted on the doors of the Hebrew houses in Egypt (Exod 12:7–8; Num 9:11).

Jesus had options, and yet he took the bread. Why? Why not another element—especially the lamb? It would seem to perfectly capture what was about to happen to him. The bread's specific meaning was the haste with which they left Egypt (flat bread, because there was no time to wait for the dough to rise; Deut 16:3). But Jesus took the bread (not the lamb) and said, "This is my body". Why?

I believe Jesus chose the bread not for its specific meaning within the Passover, but because bread stands for the entire meal. Today we might arrange to meet for 'coffee', even though the participants may choose tea or cold drinks. In many Asian cultures, an invitation to 'eat rice' is not a specific comment about what's on the menu, but a general invitation to share food. In the Bible, 'breaking bread' is about sharing a meal (Acts 2:42, 20:7), not about joining forces in literally dismembering an innocent loaf of sourdough.

When Jesus broke the bread and said, "This is my body", the "this" in that sentence is the whole Passover meal, not the bread in isolation. In communion services, the leader will sometimes say that Jesus said, "This is my body *broken* for you". This reinforces the idea that the bread is standing for his body, a picture of broken flesh. But this is not what Jesus said.[4] He said, "This is my body given for you" (Luke 22:19). Indeed, the Bible makes a point of the fact that Jesus' body was *not* broken in the process of crucifixion. In the last supper, the breaking of the bread doesn't carry the primary symbolic significance. It is a practical step so that each of those at the table can eat some of it. Just as a birthday party is not constituted by the mere presence of a cake, but also requires candles, a song and three "hip-hip hoorays!", so too the breaking of the bread alone does not carry the meaning. It is a reference to the entire Passover meal.

4 The King James Version of the Bible renders 1 Corinthians 11:24 "this is my body which is *broken* for you". But this is based on a less reliable manuscript tradition. Most modern Bible translations reflect what is likely the original text: "This is my body, which is for you" (NIV).

> Then he took a cup, and when he had given thanks, he gave it to them, saying, "Drink from it, all of you." (Matt 26:27)

The cup is an obvious symbol of Jesus' blood. What they drank was undoubtedly wine, and the suitability of wine as a picture of blood is clear. Yet it is interesting that Jesus' emphasis falls on the cup itself as much as on the contents of the cup: "Drink *from it*, all of you ..." (Matt 26:27).

Most likely, everyone had their own cup. But at this point in the meal, Jesus says in effect, "Hey, everyone! Drink from *this* cup—*my* cup". Where the breaking of the bread is a practicality more than symbolic, the sharing of the cup does carry symbolic weight. Why? Because it's *his* blood! The invitation is not for all of them to shed their blood, but to share in the benefits of his blood, shed for them. It is a symbolic way of stating the truth that salvation is in Christ alone.

The cup's contents are, of course, also full of meaning:

> "This is my blood of the covenant, which is poured out for many for the forgiveness of sins." (Matt 26:28)

In the story of the exodus, several chapters on from the events of the Passover itself, Moses gathers the people. There's a sacrifice of bulls, with half the blood being splashed against the altar and the other half being sprinkled on the people. And Moses says to them: "This is the blood of the covenant" (Exod 24:8). Israel, you see, were God's covenant people. They had entered into an agreement with God to be God's people and to shine the light of God to the world.

What is a covenant? Essentially, it's a formal agreement between two parties. Such a covenant normally involves a promise and a sign. A wedding ring, signing a piece of paper, or even handshakes are all in their own ways signs of a covenant. Covenants also involve a statement of the consequences should one party break the covenant. Covenants promise blessings to those who keep them, and curses to those who break them.

Israel had a covenant to be God's people, to live under God's law, and to show forth God's glory to the world. The consequence for breaking the covenant was exile and death; they would be cast out of the land that God was to give them. Back in Exodus, "the blood of the covenant" is, among other things, probably a sign that the consequence for breaking the covenant is death. At the last supper, Jesus says, "This is the blood of the covenant ... drink from it all of you". Just as Moses implicated everyone by sprinkling them all with the blood, Jesus implicates everyone by having them drink from his cup.

Israel had broken the covenant. Many years before Jesus came, they had received from God the promised punishment for covenant-breaking: exile. They had, to be sure, returned to the land. Well, some of them had. The truth is that, even since the exile to Babylon in the early part of the sixth century BC, most Jewish people had lived outside the land. And for those who had returned, they now lived under Roman occupation. God had promised in Jeremiah and Ezekiel that a new covenant—a new agreement between God and the people—was coming, and that in that new agreement their sins would be wiped out. Their exile would end. They would return to God, and they would receive God's Spirit. Jesus is saying that in his death, that time has now come. The curse of covenant-breaking would fall on Jesus. And in Jesus, a new covenant would be made.

From slavery to freedom

We should pay particular attention to Jesus' own interpretation of his death. What conclusions can we draw on the meaning of the death of Jesus from the last supper? I want to highlight three.

First, if I'm correct that Jesus was in effect saying, "this whole meal is about to be fulfilled in my death", then understanding the Passover is the key to understanding Jesus' death. Consider a router for an entire family's home internet connection. Everything goes through it. The Passover is the perfect router. Freedom, worship, sacrifice, victory, membership, trust, covenant—all the strands of Old Testament hope and longing come through the Passover. It's all there. Jesus, I believe, is saying that about his death too: it's all there.

Second, the meal established its participants as the new people of God. A festival like Yom Kippur was for atonement, the Feast of Tabernacles was for thanksgiving, and the Feast of Booths (also called Pentecost) was for the giving of the Law. All of them are vital aspects of Jewish theology and the Old Testament story. But the Passover alone—then and now—was the feast by which Israel said, "This is us—this is what constitutes us as a people". Passover was Israel's God-given festive answer to the question "Who are we?" The answer: Israel is the people who were brought from slavery in Egypt to be God's freed people.

If Jesus chose the meal that told Israel who they were, it follows that the last supper was the meal that told Jesus' followers who they were. It tells us who we are. We are the people who have been brought from slavery to freedom through the death of Jesus.

Third, if this is the meal by which Jesus interpreted his death, it points to the status of those who have trusted in Jesus as people who have been set free. Freedom *from* slavery, but also freedom *to* worship God.

The importance of this can be easily overlooked. We sometimes cast the story of the gospel as a simple two-act, before-and-after, bad-and-good story. In the crudest form of this story, Act One says that we were sinners, and Act Two says that God in his grace decided to forgive us through Jesus' death. As a simple table, it looks like this:

Act 1	Act 2
BAD	GOOD
We are sinners.	Jesus died for us.

Both of those things—we are sinners, and Jesus died for us—are true, but they are in fact the second and third acts of a much grander four-act story. In Act One, we were created by God as his image bearers. In Act Two, we rebelled and became sinners. In Act Three, Jesus by his death, resurrection, ascension and pouring out of the Spirit made us free—free to worship God, to put off the old self, to escape slavery to sin, and to live a new life as we await Act Four: his final coming kingdom.

Act 1	Act 2	Act 3	Act 4
GOOD	BAD	BETTER	BEST
We are created as God's image bearers.	We become sinners.	Jesus died for us. We are the new people of God, being transformed and awaiting his final kingdom.	God's kingdom comes on earth as in heaven.

Put more simply, the story goes 'Good', 'Bad', 'Better' and 'Best'. The Passover locates us in 'Better'. The death of Jesus, which has not yet ushered in the new creation ('Best'), has nevertheless dealt the decisive blow against the world, the flesh and the devil ('Better'). The cross of Jesus has genuinely changed our circumstances, such that we are, in a very real sense, free. We have been forgiven. We have peace with God. We experience the first fruits of the blessings of the coming age—even while we still cry (as the Jewish communities often do at Passover), "Next year, Jerusalem!"

Chapter 2

THE GARDEN OF TEARS

Time: Thursday 2 April, 33 AD, after dinner, late at night
Place: Garden of Gethsemane

Facing the dragon

> It was at this point that Bilbo stopped. Going on from there was the bravest thing he ever did. The tremendous things that happened afterward were as nothing compared to it. He fought the real battle in the tunnel alone, before he ever saw the vast danger that lay in wait. (JRR Tolkien, *The Hobbit*)[5]

5 JRR Tolkien, *The Hobbit: Or there and back again*, Unwin, 1981, p 205.

In *The Hobbit*, Bilbo Baggins must enter a cave, confront a dragon, and fulfil his mission. As is often the case in a hero's quest, he must confront his own fear before confronting the enemy itself. Indeed, the confrontation with the enemy itself is often not nearly as challenging as the prior decision to keep moving towards that moment of confrontation. "Going on from there was the bravest thing he ever did."

Jesus has precisely this sort of moment. He has it in the garden of Gethsemane, the garden of tears. This is Jesus' "cave"—the place in which he confronts the dragon and takes perhaps his most important step towards fulfilling his mission.

Jesus in the Garden was a 'problem passage' for the early church. From the very beginning, Christians have insisted that Jesus is God: God become man, God incarnate. But if that's true, then what's happening here in the Garden? A God who prays? A God who asks that God's will be done? A God who is anxious and afraid? How does that even work?

For many, the scene in Gethsemane was proof positive that Jesus wasn't God. Perhaps he wasn't even a great man. Jesus is not the first man to face his death, of course—it comes to us all, and most of us fear it to some extent. But many people—whether religious or not—face their death with dignity and courage. Jesus, on the other hand, faces his death with an apprehension that many others seem to avoid.

You'll recall, Jesus is not facing the ravages of cancer or ageing—awful though those are. He's a leader, a prophet—a man about to be killed for what he believes in. He's not the first such leader. In the very recent history of Jesus' Israel, the Maccabean revolutionaries faced their deaths with courage and conviction. Since the death of Jesus, many of his followers have died for their faith in him with almost super-human bravery. Even in the pagan world, stories of dignified deaths (one thinks of Socrates) were told to inspire and fortify. And yet here is Jesus, overwhelmed by what is about to happen to him, pleading that he might be spared.

But rather than being an embarrassment, I think the scene in the garden of Gethsemane is a clue—a vital clue—for answering the question that is driving this book: "Why did Jesus die?"

Overwhelmed with sorrow

> Then Jesus went with his disciples to a place called Gethsemane, and he said to them, "Sit here while I go over there and pray." (Matt 26:36)

Jesus was a man of prayer. He prayed regularly, and he taught others to pray—most famously in the Lord's Prayer. There's nothing unusual in the thought that Jesus would now take time to pray. But events take an unusual turn. Taking his three closest friends with him, he becomes "overwhelmed with sorrow to the point of death", and he asks his friends to stay and keep watch with him (Matt 26:37–38). He's not overwhelmed with sorrow *at* death—that is, at the thought that he is about to die. What he means is: "the sorrow I am carrying feels like it will kill me". He feels as if he is being drowned by sorrow.

Some of us will have known a sorrow of this calibre. The sort of sorrow that feels like it's swallowing you into the darkness. The sorrow that engulfs and suffocates. That feels like it is about to drag you under and into the grave. The claustrophobia of inescapable darkness. Jesus is saying he feels like that.

We've never seen Jesus like this before. *They've* never seen Jesus like this before. It must look to them (and it looks to us) as if Jesus is—and I don't know how better to phrase this—not coping.

Do you remember the first time you saw your dad cry? This will depend a bit on the kind of family you came from and the kind of dad you had. But for lots of families, the whole point of dads is that they cope. When you're a kid, dads just seem so strong. And by their strength, you gather the feeling that things are going to be okay, because he's okay. But one day, you find your dad crying, or not coping, or diagnosed with something that will end his life. As a child, everything you think is true and makes this world safe and good is brought into question.

Something like that must be going on for the disciples. Jesus' shoulder was the one *they* cried on. He's the one who said to them, "Come to me, all you who are weary and burdened, and I will give you rest" (Matt 11:28). He's the one whose job it was to cope, so that they knew everything was going to be okay.

But now, the one who had told them time and time

again "I've got this" is saying, "I haven't got this. Stay here and keep watch with me" (see Matt 26:38). When he comes back to them, they've fallen asleep and he pleads with them, "Couldn't you men keep watch with me for one hour?" (v 40). They had one job. And they couldn't even be there for him in his greatest hour of need. Everything they thought was true, everything that made their world seem safe, was being brought into question.

The cup and the prayer

> "My Father, if it is possible, may this cup be taken from me." (Matt 26:39)

The focus of Jesus' prayer is not a general prayer that he be saved from death, but a specific prayer that he be saved from drinking "the cup". The cup is an Old Testament picture of God's wrath. In the book of Isaiah, for example, the prophet is declaring that judgement is coming on Jerusalem for her sins. Note the language:

> Awake, awake!
> Rise up, Jerusalem,
> you who have drunk from the hand of the LORD
> the cup of his wrath ... (Isa 51:17)

Do you see? Here is the difference between Jesus and Socrates, Jesus and the martyrs, Jesus and those who would die in his name after him. They looked to their deaths and saw pain, suffering and costly faithfulness. But Jesus alone looked toward his death and saw all the sin and guilt of man, all the weight of God's holy anger against violence, unfaithfulness, injustice, perversion, cruelty, inhumanity and unholiness. All of that was what he was about to experience in his death. That was the cup he was to drink.

When you understand the meaning of the cup, the prayer of Jesus in the Garden is not embarrassing. It is extraordinary.

For one thing, it's a prayer. This is not Jesus talking to someone else *about* God. This is Jesus talking *to* God, to his Father, about the cup. There is an enormous difference between complaining *about* God and complaining *to* God. Complaining about God in the Bible is always faithless, disobedient, wicked. But the Bible's solution to complaining about God is not a stiff upper lip and a "mustn't grumble" attitude. It is, rather, to take our complaints about God and address them to God, to ask God to consider our lament (see Ps 5:1). This is what the Lord Jesus does here.

Notice also the form of the prayer: "My Father, if it is possible, may this cup be taken from me". The prayer places no conditions on God; it contains no threat of disobedience. It is not an "if/then" prayer—"Father, if you take this cup from me, then I will [insert lavish offer of obedience here]". He submits himself to the will of his Father, resolved to drink the cup that you and I deserve. The battle was won on the cross because the battle was won in the Garden. Going on from there was the bravest thing he ever did.

The lessons of the Garden

There must have been an awkwardness for the disciples as they watched Jesus face this battle. They must have asked themselves, "What are we doing here?"

It's a good thing for us as readers of the Gospels to ask the same question. Matthew's Gospel takes a camera into the Garden and keeps it rolling even when things get awkward. Why has he taken us here? What does he want us to learn? These three things at least:

1. God with us

The Gospel of Matthew opens with Jesus being given the name, "Immanuel (which means 'God with us')" (Matt 1:23). It ends with Jesus saying, "I am with you always" (Matt 28:20).

Central to Matthew's account of Jesus is an affirmation that God is not too proud to be God *with us*. The Garden shows us how dramatically *with us* God is willing to be. He knows what it is to be abandoned by friends. He knows what it is to be alone. He knows what it is to be afraid.

The letter to the Hebrews says of Jesus:

> For we do not have a high priest who is unable to empathize with our weaknesses, but we have one who has been tempted in every way, just as we are—yet he did not sin. (Heb 4:15)

If you have been lonely, betrayed, or afraid, then in the mystery of the incarnation of the Son of God, God in Christ has been there with you.

2. God instead of us

The apostle Paul reflects on the reality of the garden of Gethsemane in these words: "God made him who had no sin to be sin for us" (2 Cor 5:21).

In the Passover, as God's judgement came on Egypt, there was a safe place to stand: in the homes that had the blood of the lamb on the door. That was the sign to the angel of death: "Pass over. Blood has already been shed here."

What the blood-marked door was for those houses, the death of Jesus is for those who trust him. To be a Christian is to stand there. It is to look at the death of Jesus and say: "That was instead of me. That cup was for me, deserved by me, but drunk by him."

3. Christ without us

Jesus was frustrated that his disciples slept. I think that was for the very human reason that he wanted their company. This was his moment of trial, and he did not want to face it alone.

But there was another reason they should not have slept. In the book of Exodus, when instructions for Passover are given, it says, "Because the LORD kept vigil that night to bring them out of Egypt, on this night all the Israelites are to keep vigil ..." (Exod 12:42). To observe the Passover, they were supposed to stay up all night. And notice why: "Because the Lord kept vigil ... to bring them out of Egypt".

In the language of Exodus, the Lord stayed awake all

night to do his work of salvation. And now, on this night, more than a thousand years after the Exodus, Jesus stayed awake all night to do his work of salvation. He did so alone. He alone stays awake, keeps vigil, to secure our salvation. The people of God, represented here by the apostles, did nothing. The disciples proved perfectly useless at the point of salvation. Jesus did that by himself, without us, and for us. This is salvation by grace alone. In the words of the hymn, “Jesus paid it all, all to him I owe”.

Chapter 3

THE SONG OF THE CROSS

Time: Friday 3 April, 33 AD, 9 am–3 pm
Place: Golgotha

The sufferer's song

When you're with people in profound suffering, the general rule is: Listen more than speak. Sometimes, well-meaning friends will volunteer their theories on what it must be like: "Oh, it must be really painful" or "You must be so angry" or "I couldn't handle what you're going through". But such attempts at points of connection are usually misguided. The better policy is just to listen—to discover what is going on for them.

I think something similar applies to the crucifixion. We can come up with theories about what it must have been like for Jesus. We might find ourselves wondering, what did it *feel* like? The whipping. The nails. The strain on the body. The thirst. The heat. What was that like? How on earth does anyone go through that? But to dwell on the physical pain is another case of telling, not listening. It's me imagining where I'd be focused. Better to listen. What did *he* feel? What was it like for *him*?

Fortunately, we are not left in the dark. When Jesus was on the cross, he told us what it was like for him. He did this through song. As with many of us, when emotions overwhelm us—in a break-up, or a death, or a loss—we reach for a song to say what prose seems inadequate to communicate. So too, Jesus. When he cried out on the cross, "My God, my God, why have you forsaken me?" (Mark 15:34), he wasn't just thinking out loud. He was quoting the opening line of a song, Psalm 22, written by King David. By quoting the opening line, I think he means to evoke the whole song.[6] The song begins:

> My God, my God, why have you forsaken me?
> Why are you so far from saving me,
> so far from my cries of anguish?

6 This is often the case with songs and poems. If someone quotes a line of a song you know, you can't help but remember the whole. The psalms in particular were very well known by Jewish people, drilled into their memories through repeated use at synagogue and temple. Some commentators have even suggested when Jesus says, "It is finished" (John 19:30) on the cross, he is alluding to the end of Psalm 22 (see verse 31). All this is to suggest that there are several good reasons to assume that when Jesus quotes the opening lines of Psalm 22, he had the whole psalm in mind.

> My God, I cry out by day, but you do not answer,
> by night, but I find no rest. (vv 1–2)

Jesus (it goes without saying) was not an atheist. He is not wondering *whether* there is a God, but why God has forsaken him. He continues to trust God. God is still his God. But he feels no compulsion to be God's public relations agent. He's not trying to spin the circumstances into a more favourable light. This is no Pythonesque 'Always Look On the Bright Side of Life'. It is humble but raw: "Why are you so far from saving me?"

Jesus' experience of asking where God is in suffering is one believers have gone through before and since. In intense suffering, people whose faith is in God have found themselves saying, "I cry out by day, but you do not answer me, by night but I find no rest". Prayer feels empty—like pulling a lever that's no longer attached to anything. Yet Jesus, through the words of David, looks beyond his present experience:

> Yet you are enthroned as the Holy One;
> you are the one Israel praises.
> In you our ancestors put their trust;
> they trusted and you delivered them.
> To you they cried out and were saved;
> in you they trusted and were not put to shame.
> (vv 3–5)

God's track record with Israel is faultless. When they trusted in God, they were never put to shame; when they cried out, they were saved. Every time.

Dying of shame

For modern readers preoccupied with the physical suffering of the cross, it is surprising to find how little it features in the Gospels. A preacher looking to give some added colour and movement to a graphic account of the death of Jesus will end up in Josephus or Tacitus. In the Gospels, they'll come up short. It may surprise you to know, for example, that none of the Gospels mention Jesus being nailed to the cross.[7] In fact, while the Gospel writers record various elements of Jesus' suffering in the lead-up to the cross—the crown of thorns, being struck by the soldiers and the like—it is striking just how simple and sparse each Gospel writer is in his description of the actual crucifixion:

> There they offered Jesus wine to drink, mixed with gall; but after tasting it, he refused to drink it. *When they had crucified him*, they divided up his clothes by casting lots. (Matt 27:34–35)

> Then they offered him wine mixed with myrrh, but he did not take it. *And they crucified him*. Dividing up his clothes, they cast lots to see what each would get. (Mark 15:23–24)

7 Of course, we know from other parts of Scripture that Jesus was nailed to the cross. Thomas insists he won't believe in the risen Lord "unless I see the nail marks in his hands and put my finger where the nails were, and put my hand into his side"—a demand Jesus meets one week later (John 20:25). In his sermon on the day of Pentecost, Peter tells his fellow Israelites that they "put [Jesus] to death by nailing him to the cross" (Acts 2:23).

> When they came to the place called the Skull, *they crucified him there*, along with the criminals—one on his right, the other on his left. (Luke 23:33)
>
> *When the soldiers crucified Jesus,* they took his clothes, dividing them into four shares, one for each of them, with the undergarment remaining. (John 19:23)

When it comes to the physical event of the crucifixion, blink and you'll miss it! The biblical emphasis is much less on the *pain* of the cross, and much more on its *shame*—how embarrassing, humiliating and degrading it was. This is also the emphasis of Psalm 22:

> All who see me mock me;
>   they hurl insults, shaking their heads.
> "He trusts in the LORD," they say,
>   "let the LORD rescue him.
> Let him deliver him,
>   since he delights in him." (vv 7–8)

Those words must have been brutal. Shameful. Bitter. A fair summary of Jesus' life is "He trusts in God" (Matt 27:43). And, say his enemies, look where that got him. But the psalm remains the song of a believer, not a sceptic.

> Yet you brought me out of the womb;
>   you made me trust in you, even at my mother's breast.
> From birth I was cast on you;
>   from my mother's womb you have been my God.
>   (vv 9–10)

Holy ground

The first part of the song is a bouncing back and forth between theology (God is faithful) and experience (this is awful). From verses 12 to 18, we enter holy ground. If ever we are given access to the heart of Jesus on the cross, it is here.

> Many bulls surround me;
> strong bulls of Bashan encircle me. (v 12)

The psalm says the lions wait to tear apart their prey (v 13). David's heart turns to wax and melts within him (v 14) as villains encircle him and his enemies divide his clothes and cast lots for his garments (v 18).

In Psalm 22, the speaker is naked (see v 18). Nakedness can be an expression of intimacy, a point at which you are truly yourself before another. In the case of sexual intimacy, with your loved and trusted spouse, that may be wonderful. But public, involuntary nakedness is the opposite. It is to lose all personal dignity. It is to lose a sense of personal identity. Our clothes express our personhood. In children's books, animals with personalities wear clothing. To be naked is to be generic. It is to have all your claims to specific personal identity laid bare. For the onlookers, nakedness exposes the empty hope of the psalmist's faith. But for the psalmist, nakedness means that faith is truly all he has left. His faith is now everything, or it is nothing. There is no in-between.

Faithful in suffering

Jesus' words "My God, my God why have you forsaken me?" have sometimes been misunderstood as a confession of doubt. They are, in fact, an affirmation of his faith. Psalm 22 makes this clear:

> But you, LORD, do not be far from me.
> You are my strength; come quickly to help me.
> Deliver me from the sword,
> my precious life from the power of the dogs.
> Rescue me from the mouth of the lions;
> save me from the horns of the wild oxen.
> (vv 19–21)

Notice the litany of salvation verbs in the second half of the psalm: *help* me, *deliver* me, *rescue* me, *save* me. God will help him, deliver him, rescue him, save him. He is so confident of this that he has a plan for what he'll do after it happens:

> I will declare your name to my people;
> in the assembly I will praise you. (v 22)

When I first got my driver's licence, my mum came with me as she needed a lift across town afterwards. It was quite the experience to do a driving test knowing that someone was so confident you'd pass they already had a plan for what you'd do afterwards (I passed!). In Psalm 22, the word translated 'assembly' is the word for 'church'. And the plan of the sufferer, even while he's still suffering, is that when God rescues him (not *if*, but *when*) he'll go straight to church, straight to the assembly of God's people, and declare God's praises to everyone. "I will declare your name to my people; in the church I will praise you". And it's going to be a cracker of a service.

On the lips of King David and his sons, all Israel has a stake in his rescue. David is Israel's king. Good news for the king is good news for the people. Their freedom is tied to his. So also with Jesus. When God rescues Jesus, we are freed in his wake. And Jesus is now our worship pastor. Unashamed to call us his brothers and sisters, he leads our worship of his Father (Heb 2:11–12, 8:1–2).

And so, between Good Friday and Easter Sunday, we await the salvation of Jesus. He went to his death, as Psalm 22 makes clear, fully confident that his Father would rescue him from the grave. It is not a choice between confidence or suffering; it is about confidence *in* suffering: "For the joy set before him [Jesus] endured the cross, scorning its shame" (Heb 12:2). The shame was real; "endured" is the right word. He really did bear the wrath of God and experience God-forsakenness. But Jesus had faith in God. And by trusting God even here, even on the cross, he proved God faithful.

Suffering, then glory

What do we learn about the cross from the song Jesus sang there? We'll have eternity to plumb those depths, but let's start by drawing two conclusions.

First, Jesus on the cross was the fulfilment of the trajectory of kingship set up in the Old Testament. Did the Old Testament say, in as many words, "the Messiah will be crucified by the Romans"? No. But the Old Testament did, again and again, set up this path from suffering to glory. David, the author of Psalm 22, knew this. He suffered before entering his glory. He trusted God to raise him up. The same happened to Israel itself. God promised them a land, a nation and blessing. But first they went down into Egypt: down, then up; suffering, then glory. When Jesus says to his disciples after the event "Did not the Messiah have to suffer these things and then enter his glory?" (Luke 24:26), he wasn't referring to a secret verse about the cross hidden somewhere in 2 Chronicles. He was referring to the repeated pattern of God with his true king: first suffering, then glory.

Second, that which is the trajectory for God's Christ is also the pattern for those who are 'in Christ': "if we are children, then we are heirs—heirs of God and co-heirs with Christ, if indeed we share in his sufferings in order that we may also share in his glory", as Paul puts it in Romans 8:17. In Christ, Psalm 22 becomes our prayer, our invitation to trust God to lead us through suffering and into his glory.

Chapter 4

THE SACRIFICIAL SYSTEM FOR DUMMIES

Digging for diamonds

Jesus' death was a sacrifice of atonement. If you're familiar with Christian teaching, this sounds like a statement from Captain Obvious. It is, however, a theological move with a high degree of difficulty. Human sacrifice was an absolute taboo in Israel. The violent death of innocent humans to appease angry gods was a feature of the religions of nations Israel was defined against. Israel rejected the practice with disgust. To suggest that Jesus' death was a sacrifice, not in the broad sense that he gave up one thing for another, but in the specific sense that his death atoned for sin and dealt with God's wrath was, to say the least, a bold move.

How did the early Christians and the authors of the New Testament end up here? How did the idea that Jesus paid for our sins and propitiated the wrath of God become not just a risky thought but the joy and wellspring of their devotion? It came about, in large part, by drawing the connection between Jesus' death and the sacrificial system of the Old Testament. To understand this, we're going to need a crash course in Old Testament sacrifice. Diamonds don't lie on the surface; you have to dig for them. In the same way, we're about to hit something spectacular, but we're going to have to dig for it.

Shovels ready? Let's go.

Sacrifice in the Old Testament

The book of Leviticus is Grand Central Station for Old Testament sacrifice. Here Israel is given instructions for the priesthood, for purity, for the use of the tabernacle (and later the much more permanent temple) and for the sacrifices. Together it constituted what I'll call Israel's 'Sin Management System'. A holy God intends to dwell with his unholy people. But for him to do so, sin and its attendant defilement need to be managed.

There were five main sacrifices and there was, it seems, a logic to the way they were presented. Let's imagine it from the perspective of the worshipper.

First, you brought the *burnt offering*, in which a whole animal was burned up to God. The worshipper, once having handed it over, never touched it again. It went up in smoke as "a burnt offering, a food offering, an aroma pleasing to the LORD" (Lev 1:9). It symbolized the worshipper offering their entire self to God. Paul has this in mind when he encourages the Romans to offer their bodies "as a living sacrifice" (Rom 12:1). Whole-of-life worship is not a New Testament innovation.

Next was the *grain offering*. This entirely vegetarian sacrifice consisted of grain, olive oil, salt and flour (Leviticus 2). Here the worshipper brought not themselves but the works of their hands to the Lord, as if bringing tribute to a king.

Third was the *sin offering* (Leviticus 4). An animal was presented before the Lord and the worshipper laid his hands on its head and slaughtered it. The priest then sprinkled the blood around the tabernacle or temple. The animal was then butchered, with some of it burnt on the altar, and the rest burnt outside the camp. The emphasis was on purification—the sin offering dealt with the defiling, guilt-inducing nature of sin.

Fourth was the *guilt offering* (Lev 7:1–10). The animal was killed, the blood was splashed on all sides of the altar, and the fat and internal organs were burned up (7:1–5). The guilt offering was focused on reparation.

Last was the *fellowship offering* (Lev 7:11–21). Sometimes called the *peace offering*, this one was a shared meal, with portions given to the Lord, to the priests, and to the worshippers themselves. This means that the system began (the burnt offering) with a meal given *to* the Lord, and ended with a meal shared *with* the Lord. Nice.

There are two things to notice. First, the whole

system was more complete, complex and rich than we sometimes suppose. Some sacrifices involved blood; some didn't. Some were for sin; others were not. Some were given to the Lord; others were shared with the Lord. And so on. A holy God dwelling with a sinful people is a complex proposition. The system reflected that.

Second, notice that the system helped us to tease out some of the complex impacts of sin itself.

Let's imagine I steal your phone. The opportunity presents itself, and I give in to the temptation. What needs to happen to put things right?

Well, first, I should give the phone back. It's not mine, it's yours. So, having given it back, are we good? According to the logic of the sacrificial system, not quite. Let's say I give it back three days later. You were three days without your phone. That would have been annoying, and perhaps consequential. What appointments might you have missed? What inconveniences did you endure as a result? What relationships were strained as you were uncontactable for that time? So, you not only need your phone back—justice requires some sort of recompense for the damage I caused.

Is return plus damages the key, then? Well, yes and no. Yes, in terms of basic justice. But according to the Bible theft wasn't only unjust; it was also polluting. It was violating. It was defiling. It was (to use a non-biblical word that captures something at the heart of Levitical thinking) gross. Sin is like running a red crayon across the face of the Mona Lisa. It's like throwing dog faeces into an Apple Store. It's like getting a Happy Meal and putting it into a blender with a glass of Grange Hermitage. It makes things unclean.

Sin, you see, is messy. It happens in an ecosystem. Its damage is rarely, if ever, contained to the thing-in-itself. It damages relationships, it violates natural laws and, as the Levitical system insists, it pollutes. It is disgusting.

In contemporary Western culture, we struggle to know what to do with this aspect of sin. As author Jonathan Haidt has argued, if morality is like tastebuds, Western culture has massively downplayed the moral tastebud for disgust. We celebrate the transgressive. We carefully police any primal expression of revulsion.[8]

Yet we know this disgusting, polluting aspect of sin to be true. The Australian Government's 2007 report into the abuse of children in remote communities was titled *Ampe Akelyernemane Meke Mekarle*. Translated, it means 'Little children are sacred'. In secular Australia, nobody flinched at the title. Little children *are* sacred, and we all know it. To harm them is not just unjust or unfair; it is vile. Disgusting. Unholy.

That's what sin is like.

The Day of Atonement and the temple

The key word for atonement in the sacrificial system is the word *kippur*. It means 'to cover'. Sin is a barrier to

8 J Haidt, *The Righteous Mind: Why good people are divided by politics and religion*, Vintage, 2013.

life with God. It needs to be covered over, to be removed, to be put out of the picture. It also needs to be *covered for*, in the way that another staff member could cover your shift for you at work. They do what you otherwise would need to do. In this sense, too, the sacrificed animal could *cover for* the worshipper.

The very centre of the whole system was Yom Kippur —the Day of Covering, the Day of Atonement.

Israel's sacrificial system recognized that humans need regular cleansing from their sin. But, just as cleaning equipment will itself need cleaning from time to time, Israel's Sin Management System needed a yearly reset. The Day of Atonement was Israel's means of purging the Sin Management System.

Three features set it apart. First, it was all-consuming. Much of the sacrificial system was managed by individuals and in families. But on Yom Kippur, the whole nation downed their tools and gathered in sacred assembly before the Lord (Lev 23:27). Second, the high priest came into focus: he stood before God on behalf of the people. This was his day. Third, the high priest entered the Most Holy Place.

At this point, we need a grasp of the tabernacle (and later the temple). It was a rectangular structure with a second, smaller rectangle inside on the far end. This smaller rectangle contained an outer room (the Holy Place) and an inner room (the Most Holy Place). Inside the Most Holy Place was the Ark of the Covenant, a gold-covered wooden box with a lid. On either side of the lid were carvings of two cherubim (warrior-angels).

Between the two angels, the lid was called the 'covering'. And on it was ... nothing. And that was the whole point. In a standard-issue pagan temple, that's where you'd put the idol. That's where the pagan god *was*. But this was Israel. Heaven is God's throne, and the earth is his footstool. The highest heavens cannot contain him. He is not represented by idols. No image can represent him. He does not dwell in temples made by human hands. When the high priest of Israel goes to be where God is, he discovers an empty place.

But here is a central tension in the Old Testament. God is everywhere, and heaven and earth cannot contain him—yet God had a postcode, a street address: he was *with Israel*. He was in the tent of meeting, right there between the Cherubim. The prophet Isaiah captures the tension:

> "LORD Almighty, the God of Israel, enthroned between the cherubim, you alone are God over all the kingdoms of the earth. You have made heaven and earth." (Isa 37:16)

"Enthroned between the cherubim ... God over all the kingdoms of the earth." God could not be contained in a temple. And yet, he graciously elected to meet Israel there.

Meeting God is a fraught exercise, an encounter of the unholy with the holy. It's like sending a man into Chernobyl. The opportunities for contamination were everywhere. The high priest had to cover himself, but he also had to 'cover' the Most Holy Place: "In this way he will make atonement for the Most Holy Place because of the uncleanness and rebellion of the Israelites, whatever their sins have been" (Lev 16:16).

Why does the Most Holy Place need atonement? Remember: to atone in this context is to purge, to cleanse, to cover over impurity. This is about purging sacred space. The uncleanness and rebellion of the Israelites infected all the way into the Most Holy Place. The radioactive contamination of sin gets in everywhere. In the process of cleansing, the tabernacle itself needed to be cleansed. Just as a dishwasher collects gunk and grime as it cleans our dishes, so too the temple apparatus needed cleansing, purging, atoning, so it could continue to do its work.

The two goats

The Day of Atonement also required a particular sacrifice of two goats: One for the Lord, and the other a 'scapegoat'. The one is sacrificed to the Lord for the sins of the people; the other is sent off into the desert.

> He is to lay both hands on the head of the live goat and confess over it all the wickedness and rebellion of the Israelites—all their sins—and put them on the goat's head. He shall send the goat away into the wilderness in the care of someone appointed for the task. The goat will carry on itself all their sins to a remote place; and the man shall release it in the wilderness. (Lev 16:21–22)

The meaning of the first goat is straightforward enough: it is a sacrifice for sin. But what of the second goat? The term used to describe this goat is usually translated "scapegoat" (Lev 16:8, 10, 26). It's literally "the goat for Azazel". But who, or what, is Azazel?

'Azazel' is likely a reference to a demon associated with the desert.[9] The desert is the place of demons, the unformed world of chaos. Where did Israel bow down to idols? The desert. Where does Jesus get tested by Satan? The desert. Why does Jesus do so much demon exorcism in the Gospels? Because he's cleansing the land. He's sending the demons, who have come into Israel via idolatry and covenant-breaking, back to where they belong. Paul, when exercising church discipline, hands people "over to Satan" (see 1 Cor 5:5; 1 Tim 1:20). He's not offering them in worship to Satan. Rather, he is casting them out of sacred space (that is, the church community) and into the realm of Satan. In other words, sin needs to be atoned for (goat number one) *and* cast out (goat number two). It needs to be paid for *and* gotten rid of—sent back to the realm of demons, where it belongs. This is at the heart of the Day of Atonement.

Israel is holy space. The tabernacle is holy-holy space. And the Most Holy Place is, well, Most Holy of All. Sin doesn't belong in sacred space. It if 'belongs'

9 To see the argument for this identification of Azazel laid out in a helpful and, to my mind, compelling way, see M Heiser, *The Unseen Realm: Recovering the supernatural worldview of the Bible*, Lexham Press, 2015, pp 176–178.

anywhere, it belongs in the wilderness, in the desert, in the unformed places, in the haunt of demons.

Don't worry, we'll get back to Jesus in the next chapter, because of course Jesus is the fulfilment of the whole system. But we need a working understanding of what that system was in order to appreciate what it was that Jesus fulfilled. The whole system was designed to manage sin. And the Day of Atonement is the 'have you tried turning it off and on again?' day.[10] It's the day when sin was purged from the very system that was there to purge sin in the first place.

This is the mental furniture with which the New Testament authors began to unpick the riddle of Jesus' death. Ideas of priests and high priests, sacrifices and offerings, holy and most holy spaces, bloodshed and bodies offered up to heaven, the Day of Atonement, and the presence of God above the Ark of the Covenant—the writers of the New Testament had all this in their heads. It was baked into how they saw the world and how they understood that a human could relate to God. Unless we know what they knew, we can't see what they saw.

What did they see? They saw the white-hot holiness of God.

The context of Leviticus 16 is important: we are told that "the LORD spoke to Moses after the death of the two sons of Aaron" (Lev 16:1). We later learn that Aaron's sons had approached God with "unauthorized fire"

10 I owe this phrase to theologian Alistair Roberts.

(Num 3:4), and by doing so were an affront to God's holiness. They worshipped God the wrong way, and they died. The threat of death hangs over the whole day. The various sacrifices of the day are all established to protect Aaron and the subsequent high priests from death through contact with the presence of God. When the unholy approaches Holiness itself, there will be blood. The wonder and the genius of the sacrificial system is that it need not necessarily be *our* blood—God, in his mercy, will accept a substitute.

They also saw the determination of God to be with his people. In Leviticus, God 'pitched his tent' with his people. He became present and made his dwelling with them. The high priest beheld his glory, the glory of the one and only, full of grace and truth (see John 1:14). God came into the toxicity of sin-infested humanity, with the tabernacle as the PPE necessary for his presence. The question was never *whether* he'd dwell with his people; the question was *how* he would dwell with his people. And the answer? Through the sacrificial system.

They also saw something about sin: it defiles. It gets in everywhere, messes up everything, affects everyone. Nathan Hobby's Young Adult novel *The Fur* tells the story of a Western Australia cut off from the rest of the world as a fungus grows and overtakes the city of Perth. Leviticus sees sin in similar terms: a growing, gross fungal-type infection. Each year the camp was purged. But each year it started to creep its way back into the Most Holy Place, like mould in an old bathroom, and needed to be purged again. Sin, as no participant in the sacrificial system could ever miss, needs radical treatment. It is not easily contained.

The sacrificial system was open to corruption. By the time of Jesus, it was beyond redeeming. The temple system, like a sketchy dishwasher, was making things worse, not better. But at its best, the sacrificial system was a powerful object lesson on the nature of sin. And it was a powerful testimony to the faithfulness of God.

A world without atonement

In our culture, we see the effects of sin everywhere. But we have no atonement. In the secular West, we don't even have the broken Sin Management Systems of other religions. We have judgement without forgiveness, guilt without atonement, defilement without cleansing. Without God, we have built a system of shame and cancel culture to rival the most devout of religious communities: Slut-shaming, revenge porn, cancellation-without-trial and the like. We are quick to judge and to shame each other, but very slow to offer forgiveness or imagine that atonement is possible. The social media pile-on is how we send sinners into the desert. No substitute is provided. There is no goat to stand in anyone's place.

Singer-songwriter Nick Cave was recently asked to describe cancel culture:

> As far as I can see, cancel culture is mercy's antithesis. Political correctness has grown to become the unhappiest religion in the world. Its once honourable

> attempt to reimagine our society in a more equitable way now embodies all the worst aspects that religion has to offer (and none of the beauty)—moral certainty and self-righteousness shorn even of the capacity for redemption. It has become quite literally, bad religion run amuck.[11]

It's like we've understood one half of the logic of the Levitical system. Look at our language: *Toxic* masculinity, *cancel* culture, the *stain* of colonialism. This sort of language draws on Levitical ideas of purity and the defiling nature of sin. But we have no system of cleansing, no mercy, no God to show up and make things better. We store up vast reservoirs of guilt and shame, with no means of covering, no mechanism of atonement.

In the Old Testament, Israel had the sacrificial system. In the New Testament, we meet him to whom the whole system was pointing. On our own, we've got nothing. In the secular West people are left to wallow in guilt and shame—or to "eat and drink, for tomorrow we die" (1 Cor 15:32). The good news is that the news of Jesus is genuinely good news. When the kids of cancel culture and the hellishness of social media's unwipeable remembrance of sins past discover the lavish, unbridled, kick-butt, glorious, forgetful, mercy-soaked, industrial-strength forgiveness of the cross of Christ, man! The kids are going to love it!

11 'What is mercy for you? What do you think of cancel culture?', *The Red Hand Files,* August 2020, accessed 14 February 2023 (theredhandfiles.com/what-is-mercy-for-you).

Chapter 5

JESUS OUR GREAT HIGH PRIEST

Like them, and better than them

As we saw in the last chapter, the high priest was front and centre on the Day of Atonement. It was his day. The congregation of Israel gathered to watch him offer his sacrifices, disappear into the Most Holy Place, and then return with the blessing of God from one who had just met with God. The high priest represented God to the people, and he represented the people to God. On no other day in Israel's religious life was their focus so singularly on one man. The nation's access to God rested on him. This old covenant practice helps us to grasp what it means when the New Testament says that Jesus is our high priest. The New Testament both compares Jesus to the high priests of the old covenant (Jesus is like them) and it contrasts Jesus to the high priest of the old covenant (Jesus is better than them). Either way, the fact that Jesus is our high priest is good news. It's especially good news for Christians facing the ongoing reality of sin in their lives. If you've ever been confused, perplexed or disappointed by the continuing presence of sin in your life, read on. This is for you. Our guide will be the letter to the Hebrews.

The context of Hebrews

Hebrews was written to a group of Jewish Christians who had come to faith in the Messiah Jesus and been following him for a while. They'd gone through a radical change in their religious patterns, including walking away from the sacrificial system. Having discovered in Jesus the reality to which the whole system pointed, the system itself was now surplus to requirements.

Things began well for these new Christians. Like many of us when we first come to Christ, there were early wins and thrilling discoveries. But fast-forward a few years, and the initial sugar rush of new life in Christ has started to wear off. At one level, that's okay. Just as falling in love can lead to marriage, which is simultaneously less intense and far deeper, the Christian life can and should settle into something deeper than the initial thrill of discovery. What's hard, though, is when some of the sins you thought you had beaten come back to haunt you. Temptations that you resisted overpower you again. Doubts that were once at bay begin to manifest. In the early days you discover a bunch of new friends, but as the months and years march on, you also discover a less welcome phenomenon: the loss of old friends. Your previous religious community, family members and friends chip away at your joy with responses of bemusement, cynicism and occasional hostility.

For the readers of Hebrews, life was once full of temple worship and liturgies and sacrifices and ceremonies and cleansing and a grand building and a whole community and religious professionals to boot. Now it's all Bible studies and house churches. That just feels different. Less tactile, less kinaesthetic—perhaps even a little bit (well, let's just say it out loud) lame.

Put that all together: old sins and temptations return, the mechanisms you once had for dealing with shame and guilt have gone, and the costs of following Jesus are rapidly increasing. You're now looking back to what you left behind, wondering if you lost something precious in the transfer. The book of Hebrews addresses an acute case of spiritual FOMO (Fear of Missing Out). The temptation to re-engage the sacrificial system is real.

What does a pastoral intervention look like in this scenario?

The book of Hebrews sets out to persuade the wavering community that what they have now is better. Jesus is the better worshipper, the better word, the bringer of a better covenant, the pioneer of a better salvation. He is the reality for which the Old Testament was the shadow, the real thing of which the Old Testament was the working model, the destination for which the Old Testament was the road sign.

And Jesus is the better high priest.

The God who never cheated

Jesus was not from a priestly family. Nor is there any record of him ever offering a sacrifice. If he'd held a passport, under 'Occupation' it would have said 'Carpenter/ Prophet'. It would not, and could not, have said 'Priest'.

And yet, according to the letter to the Hebrews, our whole salvation rests on the conviction that Jesus is not just *a* priest, but *the* great high priest to which all priesthood in the Old Testament points. He both fulfils and transcends the Old Testament vision of priesthood.

The Old Testament priests were selected from the people and appointed by God. Both elements matter: they needed to be from the people because they represented the people to God; and they needed to be appointed by God in order to represent God to the people. On both criteria, Jesus passes.

But then there's a tricky one: the high priest of the Old Testament was able to deal gently with people because "he himself [was] subject to weakness" (Heb 5:2). Surely Jesus doesn't fit this criterion. So, should we accept, with Meatloaf, that "two out of three ain't bad"? Or was Jesus, like them, subject to weakness after all? The surprising answer of Hebrews is yes, Jesus was indeed subject to weakness.

> During the days of Jesus' life on earth, he offered up prayers and petitions with fervent cries and tears to the one who could save him from death, and he was heard because of his reverent submission. Son though

he was, he learned obedience from what he suffered ... (Heb 5:7–8)

This is a surprise to many Christians, but it's crucial. The best way I can put it is this: when God became human in Jesus, he never cheated. Not once. Not ever.

Many of us have this view of Jesus as a 'human'—wink, wink, nudge, nudge. He was a 'man', but a man in the manner of a poorly written superhero character who has infinite powers and therefore will win any battle. This version of Jesus had 'struggles' and 'temptations', but not real struggles. Puberty was a breeze; the devil didn't stand a chance in the wilderness. And at the prospect of his death, he was probably thinking, "how bad can it be? What—three days, max? I've got this!"

But here's the thing: when God did humanity in Jesus, he went all in. He never cheated. Not once. Not ever.

Jesus Christ, the incarnate second person of the Trinity, learned God the way we do—by reading his Bible. He *grew* in knowledge of God and *learned* obedience (Heb 5:8; Luke 2:40, 46, 52). He used Scripture when facing temptation (Matt 4:7) and for comfort (Matt 27:46), just as we do. He lived dependent on every word that comes from the mouth of God (Matt 4:4). Imagine that—the second person of the Trinity became human and then learned about God his Father by reading his Bible, just like us. He never cheated. Not once. Not ever.

He prayed. He prayed to God with "with fervent cries and tears" (Heb 5:7). He who was the light of life submitted himself to the darkness of death. He entrusted himself to his Father, but his perfect obedience to God didn't just come with his factory settings. It was something he learned—through suffering.

Jesus never sinned. The difference between him and us is not that we are tempted and he wasn't. We are both tempted. The difference is that he never gave in. Imagine living at that level of intensity! As CS Lewis points out, not giving into temptation makes your encounter with sin more, not less, difficult.

> A silly idea is current that good people do not know what temptation means. This is an obvious lie. Only those who try to resist temptation know how strong it is. After all, you find out the strength of the German army by fighting against it, not by giving in. You find out the strength of a wind by trying to walk against it, not by lying down. A man who gives in to temptation after five minutes simply does not know what it would have been like an hour later. That is why bad people, in one sense, know very little about badness—they have lived a sheltered life by always giving in. We never find out the strength of the evil impulse inside us until we try to fight it: and Christ, because He was the only man who never yielded to temptation, is also the only man who knows to the full what temptation means—the only complete realist.[12]

Jesus is our real and sympathetic high priest. He knows temptation more intimately than we do—not despite the fact that he never gave in to it, but *because* he never

12 CS Lewis, *Mere Christianity*, Harper Collins, 1977, p 123.

gave in to it. Not once. Not ever.

Most Protestant churches (including mine) avoid the word 'priest' for the person exercising pastoral oversight. I think that's good. I don't want to be called a priest. I don't offer sacrifices to God, I don't wear special clothes, and my vows are the vows of my baptism: to follow Jesus and trust him for my whole life.

But we Protestants get it wrong when we think we don't have priests because we don't need priests—when we think we can handle the God thing all by ourselves. A direct line, us and God, working it out just between the two of us. No religious apparatus for us, thanks! We like it nice and simple.

No! Christianity is a mediated religion. There is no independent access to God. Never has been and never will be. Any time we approach God, the question is never: "Do you need a priest?" The question is: "*Which priest* do you need?" The answer (of course) is Jesus. Jesus is the high priest we need.

The high priests went into the earthly tabernacle; Jesus went into the heavenly one (Heb 9:11). The high priests went into the presence of God once a year; Jesus lives there (Heb 7:24–25). The high priests had to deal with their own sins first; Jesus, who never sinned, deals with our sins (Heb 7:27). The high priests prayed for the people; Jesus prays for us constantly (Heb 7:24–25). What's Jesus doing right now? Answer: he is praying for you. True story.

Approaching the throne of grace

A little while ago, I went and saw a counsellor to help me work through a few things I'd got stuck on. I hadn't really done that before. A little nervous, I decided to dress up. Best shirt with collar, grown-up trousers and my smartest shoes. I wanted people to look at me in the lobby and think: "Wow! He's really got it together." I even wanted the counsellor to think: "Gee! This guy is very on top of stuff." If I was going to get diagnosed as crazy, I wanted to be high-functioning crazy.

It was really silly. Who goes to a professional therapist trying to give the impression they don't need a professional therapist? They're a therapist! They are trained to help you. They expect you not to be well. They will be unshockable, able to help bring you up out of your weakness. If you're ever going to let yourself be vulnerable, this is the time. Going for help and then acting like we don't need help is, frankly, a bit weird.

Sometimes we are like this with Jesus. We come to him, all suited up, hoping that he'll think: "Man, this guy hardly needs me! Well done, you!"

Here's the good news: Jesus is onto you. He knows what you're up against. He knows how hard temptation is. He knows what it is to go through puberty. To lose friends. To fear death. To feel pain. To trust God when everything is falling apart. He's a really good high priest. Therefore, go to him. Don't get dressed up first. Don't try and get things in order before you show up. Approach him with confidence. He's been there too. He knows what it's like. He's not holding it over you. He's not annoyed that you came. He loves you. He's here (by his Spirit) and there (at the right hand of the Father) because he wants to help.

Chapter 6

JESUS OUR SACRIFICE

One for many?

Priests offer sacrifices. It's a non-negotiable of the job. According to the New Testament, Christ our priest was also Christ the priestly sacrifice. In his death on the cross, he was the lamb laid down for the sins of the world (John 1:29; Rev 5:9). But this raises at least two questions we need to consider. First, how does one death pay for the sins of many? Psalm 49 indicates that even one life paying for another life is tricky: "No one can redeem the life of another or give to God a ransom for them—the ransom for a life is too costly, no payment is ever enough" (Ps 49:7–8). And second, if (as we will discover) the sacrifice of Jesus is qualitatively greater than any other sacrifice, what does that mean for assurance? Does a greater sacrifice mean a greater confidence in salvation than was available to Old Testament believers? Is it once saved, always saved?

For some answers, we'll turn again to our old friend, the book of Hebrews.

A better temple

The first readers of Hebrews were looking backward to the temple and the sacrificial system they had left behind. With no more sacrifices, had they lost something precious? The writer of Hebrews assures them the temple was a "copy and shadow of what is in heaven" (Heb 8:5). Jesus went into the better temple. Copies and shadows can be very impressive. Some doll's houses, for example, take on the status of an art form. Some even have little beds made up with actual linen. The proportions are so perfect and the detail so exquisite—an almost perfect copy of a real house.

But still only a copy.

The temple was like that. Israel's temple was brilliant. It was amazing. It was God-given. But it was only ever a shadow and copy of the heavens. The high priest would disappear from the crowd and go, on behalf of the people, into the Holy of Holies. When Christ 'disappeared', he "went through the greater and more perfect tabernacle that is not made with human hands" (Heb 9:11). That's where Jesus is now, in the reality of the throne room of God, ministering in the better temple—the true temple of which the earthly temple was only a copy.

A better sacrifice

> He did not enter by means of the blood of goats and calves; but he entered the Most Holy Place once for all by his own blood ... (Heb 9:12)

The Old Testament system was not arbitrary. It really was God's provision for sin. But it worked by pointing beyond itself. The blood of bulls and goats could not take away sin (Heb 10:4). They were outward signs for outward cleansing. They could only ever point towards the real cleansing that was to come through the sacrifice of Jesus (Heb 10:10). Jesus offers himself—not animal blood, but his own blood; not the life of a beast, but the life of a fellow human; not the body of an unblemished animal, but the life of an unblemished man.

This brings us to one of the central questions on the death of Jesus: How does one man's death pay for the sins of the whole world? If we approach it mathematically, shouldn't it be one-for-one—one life for one life? How does one pay for the sins of many?

The one-for-many principle is a mainstay of biblical thinking. Heads of state, heads of families, high priests and so on—the one stands in representative relationship for the many all the time. On the Day of Atonement, the high priest stood in for the people. He represented them to God. Jesus stands not just as a man, but as a *representative* man. Head of the family, priest for the people, king of the nation.

As we've already noted, the physical suffering of Jesus is a surprisingly muted aspect of the Gospel accounts of his death. It is certainly never put forward in the Bible to explain the extent of the atonement. Irish theologian TC Hammond put it this way:

> The work of Christ is not merely a substitute for an equivalent unfulfilled work of the sinner. It has in itself an intrinsic value ... The value of Christ's sacrifice consisted in the infinite worth of his person.[13]

The point is not how bad his suffering was; the point is *who suffered*: it happened to Jesus, the God-Man. Jesus, the one who knew no sin. Jesus, the one who lived faithfully before God at every point. Jesus, who never cheated, never deviated from the path of faithful obedience to the Father. Jesus, who was in very nature God but did not consider equality with God something to be used for his own advantage (see Phil 2:6). It is the infinite value of his person that makes his sacrifice effective for all.

The lid of the ark

Remember that lid (mentioned in chapter 4) on top of the ark? The place where there was no idol? The place where sinful man and a holy God could be present to each other? That idea appears again in the New Testament, but notice what happens:

13 TC Hammond, *In Understanding Be Men: A handbook of Christian doctrine* (DF Wright ed), revised edn, IVP, 1968, p 120.

> God presented Christ as a *sacrifice of atonement* [the same word used for the lid of the ark] through the shedding of his blood—to be received by faith. He did this to demonstrate his righteousness, because in his forbearance he had left the sins committed beforehand unpunished—he did it to demonstrate his righteousness at the present time, so as to be just and the one who justifies those who have faith in Jesus. (Rom 3:25–26)

In the past, God left sin unpunished. Of course, some sins are punished some of the time. But taken as a whole, the one-to-one connection between sin and punishment is not a feature of this world. People sin and get away with it. We are not treated as our sins deserve. Some suffering is not because of sin (John 9:1–3), and much sin does not result in suffering in this world. We tend to think that we just happen to live in that sort of universe. But the truth is not that we live in that sort of universe, but we live in a universe governed by *that sort of God*. God is merciful. He is patient and longsuffering. He does not treat us as our sins deserve. Every time we sin and are not punished, we experience God's mercy.

What of his righteousness? What of his holiness? His utter opposition to sin and to evil? In the old covenant, as we have seen, God provided the tabernacle. In the tabernacle he provided the Most Holy Place. In the Most Holy Place was the ark. And on the ark, God provided the lid of the ark, the mercy seat, the place of atonement. It was accessible only by blood. Only as the animals were sacrificed in place of the people could the high priest enter and meet with God. The lid of the ark, in other words, was a demonstration of God's mercy (because it expressed God's determination to meet with sinful man) and his righteousness (because sin was, symbolically, punished). But in Jesus, fully and finally, the true sacrifice is made. God has set forth Jesus as the place where justice and mercy kiss—the place where God simultaneously is "just *and* the one who justifies those who have faith in Jesus".

This is good news! Through the blood of Jesus, sin in all its toxicity has been dealt with. And this is open for everyone. Literally everyone. The New Testament makes this connection straight away. If on the cross God is both just and the one who justifies those who have faith in Jesus, then there is no space for me saying, "I'm slightly better than you because I required less from God to have my sins dealt with" (Rom 3:27). Not true! We all come in the same way, on the same basis, at the same cost to God (his Son), and with the same out-of-pocket expenses for us (absolutely none).

By this, God is God not only of the Jews, but of the Gentiles too (Rom 3:30). If "Jews and Gentiles alike are all under the power of sin" (Rom 3:9), then there is no difference between Jew and Gentile. Both are sinners in the same way, and both are justified freely by grace through the same redemption that came through the same Jesus (Rom 3:23). This means, gloriously, that the doors to God's mercy are wide, wide open. As Susannah Black Roberts put it in a recent tweet:

> Christianity is a religion of and for vicious meth heads and MAGA chuds and annoying pink haired woke activists and TERFs and Brooklyn wine moms and nice bourgeois Dave Ramsey-abiding debt free suburbanites and that is just kinda wild. Errybody git in that water.[14]

It is wild. And it's fantastic! Come on, errybody git in that water!

Assurance and warning

The New Testament takes the complete nature of Christ's sacrifice in two seemingly opposite directions: it serves both as a warning and an assurance. The warning is: this sacrifice is God's provision for sin. There's no plan B, so don't walk away. And the assurance is: this sacrifice is God's provision for sin. There's no need for a plan B. Salvation is here.

Let's start with the warning. This one is taken from Hebrews 10. And, fair warning, it's terrifying.

> If we deliberately keep on sinning after we have received the knowledge of the truth, no sacrifice for sins is left, but only a fearful expectation of judgement and of raging fire that will consume the enemies of God. Anyone who rejected the law of Moses died

14 Susannah Black Roberts, 'Christianity is a religion of and for vicious meth heads ...' [Tweet], @suzania, 3 June 2022, accessed 15 February 2023 (twitter.com/suzania/status/1532445501840310272).

> without mercy on the testimony of two or three witnesses. How much more severely do you think someone deserves to be punished who has trampled the Son of God underfoot, who has treated as an unholy thing the blood of the covenant that sanctified them, and who has insulted the Spirit of grace? ... It is a dreadful thing to fall into the hands of the living God. (Heb 10:26–29, 31)

It couldn't be starker. Notice the logic: in Christ, we have a greater salvation. A better high priest. A more perfect sacrifice. Access to the true temple. But because what we have is better, the stakes are higher. If there were consequences under the old covenant for faithlessness, how much more under the new and better covenant? If there were punishments for treating as unholy items in the tabernacle, which was a copy and shadow, then how much more for trampling the Son of God underfoot?

Holding onto Jesus

But what of assurance? Is it "once saved, always saved"? Or could a Christian fall away?

The problem, I think, is in the framing of the question. Where do the statement "once saved, always saved" and the question "can a Christian fall away?" point me? They point me back to a moment of salvation. They point me, in other words, to *me*. This type of thinking encourages me to answer the question "will I be saved?" by asking the question "was I once saved?" But that's a bad question. For it encourages either self-confidence or self-doubt—self-confidence because I am now resting on my prior conversion experience, or self-doubt because I can always wonder how real that experience was.

The book of Hebrews presents a better way. It doesn't direct us to ourselves, but to *Christ and his sacrifice*. And it doesn't direct us back to a past event in our lives. Instead, it asks us how we are presently relating to Jesus and his death. Both the warning and the assurance are addressed with the same truth about the death of Jesus for us.

Imagine you're about to board a ship to, let's say, Singapore. It's a big ship from a company with a pristine safety record. These guys are on it. Totally safe. You're going to be just fine. But you're a little nervous. So, as you board, you ask the captain: "Will we be safe on this ship?"

"Yep, completely safe! This ship has been tested in the roughest of seas. It can withstand the most challenging weather. It's delivered thousands of people safely to their destination. We've triple-checked everything. Safety is our number one value and highest concern. On this ship, you will be safe."

"So, even if I get off this ship, I won't drown?"

Wait, what?!

"No, I'm talking about the ship", says the captain. "Stay on the ship. That's where you're safe. I wasn't saying anything about your ability to survive in the open sea. You won't be safe there. I was talking about the ship. This is where you'll be safe."

It is like that with Jesus. His blood has washed away our sins. He is in heaven praying for us. He will never abandon us. He will hold us to the end. Therefore, stay on this ship! Stick with Jesus and his sacrifice!

Assurance and warning, then, are two sides of the same coin. Jesus is where salvation is. Stay with him, and you'll be safe. Abandon him, and you will discover that "it is a dreadful thing to fall into the hands of the living God". The assurance we have is about Jesus, not about our ability to swim on our own.

> Therefore, brothers and sisters, since we have confidence to enter the Most Holy Place by the blood of Jesus, by a new and living way opened for us through the curtain, that is, his body, and since we have a great priest over the house of God, let us draw near to God ... (Heb 10:19–22)

Come with confidence. The ticket to Singapore doesn't confer on you a personal ability to survive the open seas, but if you stay on the ship you can be sure of the destination. Similarly, in Jesus I can be utterly confident of my destination. Our role is to hold onto him, to remain in him.

Among Christians, there is a particular sort of introspective, earnest person who will find a way to steal insecurity from the jaws of assurance, despair from the clutches of joy. Such a person will circle down into unsolvable puzzles and unwinnable internal debates:

Have I trusted God enough? Am I actually 'on the boat', or am I only imagining it? When I'm told to "hold on" to Jesus, how hard should I be holding? Is there a particular grip he prefers? What if I'm only holding on with one hand? What about when I'm asleep? Or concentrating on my work? What about when an old, seemingly beaten sin comes back to haunt me? What about when I doubt? Can you simultaneously be holding onto Jesus and wondering if God is real? What are the other guys doing? Is their "holding on" different from mine? Do their prayers feel more real? Is their faith more faithy?

Can I speak frankly, one over-thinker to another? This is not rocket science. You're overthinking it. Just trust him! Hold onto him! That's all. Look to him. Don't look at yourself looking to him. Don't take selfies of yourself holding onto him. Just hold onto him. We are saved by grace, not by intensity. We are saved by faith in him, not by faith in our faith in him. In the trenches of everyday life, this looks an awful lot like saying your prayers, reading your Bible, meeting with God's people, confessing your sins and slowly growing in holiness. It coexists with running out of toothpaste, having a bad hair day and forgetting where you parked your car.

Instead of overthinking, you could simply pray like Sir Jacob Astley (1579–1652): "O Lord, Thou knowest how busy I must be this day. If I forget Thee, do not thou forget me." That's a good prayer. Trust him. Say your prayers. And get on with living your life in the love of God. God really does love you. As Paul reminds us in Romans, "God demonstrates his own love for us in this: While we were still sinners, Christ died for us" (Rom 5:8). Think about that. He loved you, and he sent Jesus to die for you, when you were his enemy. Do you really think he's going to let you down now that you and God are friends and Jesus is raised to life? You'll be fine. Trust him. He's got you. He's really good at this sort of thing.

Chapter 7

IN OUR PLACE CONDEMNED HE STOOD

How the cross deals with our guilt

Who could disagree?

Some years ago at our church, we asked our trainees to read JI Packer's classic essay 'What Did the Cross Achieve? The logic of penal substitution'.[15] In this essay, the great British theologian sets out a careful, nuanced and compelling case for the penal substitutionary nature

15 This essay is available in numerous places online, including the 9 Marks website (9marks.org/article/what-did-the-cross-achieve-the-logic-of-penal-substitution). It is also included in full in Packer's book (co-authored with Mark Dever) *In My Place Condemned He Stood: Celebrating the Glory of the Atonement* (Crossway, 2008).

of Christ's work on the cross. I was excited for them to read it.

They were underwhelmed.

They did not find any fault with the writing, or the exegesis, or the theology as such. Rather, the trainees were perplexed because, for them, it was hard to make sense of what Packer was arguing *against*. Christ died in our place to take the penalty for our sins—who's on the other side of this issue? Here was Packer carefully defending a position they had no idea needed defending. It was like reading an earnest essay defending the existence of gravity.

Penal substitutionary atonement is a bit like that. In the academy and among Christian leaders, the idea is controversial, contentious and occasionally used as a tribal boundary marker. Denominations and ministries have split over the issue. Vast quantities of ink have been poured out in its defence, or in an effort to bring about its defeat. Conscientious believers (such as Packer) have set out to explain the doctrine in a manner that rescues it from what they regard as clumsy presentations. Meanwhile, as these theological armies clash by night, the average Christian can be found cheerfully belting out the truth that "on the cross, as Jesus died, the wrath of God was satisfied", unaware of all the fuss.

This state of blissful ignorance has much to commend it. But you're in the middle of a book on the cross. If we're ever going to dig into this idea, this is the place to do it. So, it's time to roll up our sleeves and explore the wonderful (and occasionally controversial) claim that Jesus died in our place to take the punishment for our sins—penal substitutionary atonement.

Christ died in our place for our sins: penal substitutionary atonement

The idea of penal substitutionary atonement is, as the name suggests, the claim that Christ's death paid a penalty (penal). As Christ did not deserve a penalty, he was paying it for others (substitutionary). And the result of Christ's paying this price for others is that we are now forgiven (atonement).

The idea of a 'penalty' takes us into the realm of the law court, the world of crime and punishment. Before the judge, the guilty party is dealt a penalty for their misdeeds, whether that be a fine, a prison sentence, or (depending on the jurisdiction) the death penalty.

Does our sin warrant a penalty? The answer (it seems almost too obvious to even have to say) is yes. God is the Judge of all the earth, and he will not leave the guilty unpunished (Exod 34:7; Num 14:18; Nah 1:3).

Notice that the law-court image means we are speaking of a judicial rather than a natural penalty. A natural penalty is when the consequence is baked into the act itself—for example, abuse of alcohol leads to bad health outcomes, reckless spending leads to poverty, and unkindness leads to a diminished social life. But in this context, the penalty means more than 'cause-and-effect in a moral universe'. It specifically refers to the idea that

God, our Judge, applies a judicial penalty to our sins.

For punishment to be just, it must also be proportional. The practice in some communities of removing a man's hand for stealing might be effective, but it is also unjust. Stealing is a sin, to be sure. But losing your hand for the rest of your life is wildly out of proportion to the sin itself.

What is the just punishment for our rebellion against God? The Bible's answer is death—physical and spiritual separation from God. God gave us life. To take his gift and reject the giver is treason. It is a capital offence: "the wages of sin is death" (Rom 6:23).

But Christ substitutes himself for us. He takes our penalty.

The idea of substitution is admittedly wide-ranging. Sometimes, as on a sports team, substitution has a one-to-one correspondence: someone comes off the field, and someone else from the bench steps in and takes their place. Other times, substitution has a more representative character: the prime minister (or president or monarch) represents us as a nation. And representation has an aspect of substitution. The one who stands for us stands where we would otherwise have needed to stand, and so substitutes for us. And the one who stands for us must be one of us. Substitution also has a solitary aspect, like the priest who walks from the people into the Most Holy Place.

All of this is in play here. But specifically, when we speak of penal substitutionary atonement, we are highlighting the 'in our place' aspect of substitution. The penalty was due to us, but it fell on Christ. And this is because he stood where we otherwise should have been and received what we otherwise should have received. On the cross, the righteous wrath of God against sin and against sinners was poured out on the one man who knew no sin, but who in that moment became sin for us (2 Cor 5:21). Through Christ, his death on the cross and subsequent resurrection, we are rescued from the wrath to come (1 Thess 1:10) because that wrath has now fallen on him.

This means we are atoned for. Because Christ substituted as our penalty and bore the wrath of God that we deserve, we are now able to stand before God guiltless. We have no case to answer, no penalty to pay, no punishment to await. This is what we mean by penal substitutionary atonement.

Objections

Depending on your background, the description above may still leave you scratching your head, wondering what possible objection it could raise. Isn't everything that's just been said what the Bible says?

Let's consider the nature of the objections that are sometimes raised.

Some of the objections come from unbelief, while some come from more fundamental objections to the Christian faith itself. Islam, for example, sees no atonement in the death of Jesus because it says that Jesus did not die at all.[16] Atheists object because there is no God whose wrath needs to be turned aside. Liberal or progressive Christians might accept this is what the Bible says, but relegate it to an early phase of human reflection on the cross from which we have since advanced.

Responding to these objections would be a worthwhile exercise in another context, but I do not want to make that our focus here. Rather, I want to focus on three questions that arise, as it were, from within the logic of penal substitution itself. These objections, if answered, will serve us in believing more intelligently and faithfully. The three objections, stated in the form of questions, are:

- Why doesn't God just forgive?
- Is substitution just?
- Is penal substitution rational?

Why doesn't God just forgive?

Why must a penalty be paid at all? God seems to require us to just forgive others, so why doesn't he do the same?

The answer is in the character of God and the nature of forgiveness. God is just. He cannot wink at sin or sweep it under the rug. To forgive without a sacrifice of atonement would be to leave sin unpunished, and so to enthrone evil.

In a powerful essay entitled 'Christianity and Violence', theologian Miroslav Volf explores the relationship

16 Qur'an 4:157–158.

between violence and religion, arguing that Christianity—rightly understood and rightly practised—fosters more peaceful social environments, not more violence. As part of this wider argument, Volf notes that a God who simply forgave—who turned a blind eye to real evil—would be a God who condoned evil. In Volf's words:

> Absolute hospitality would in no way amount to absence of violence. To the contrary, it would enthrone violence precisely under the guise of nonviolence because it would leave the violators unchanged and the consequences of violence unremedied.[17]

The choices are stark: Either God ignores the cries of the oppressed for justice and so condones the perpetrators, or he punishes evil and in so doing closes the door on forgiveness. The genius of the cross is that it achieves both. In it, God is *both* "just *and* the one who justifies those who have faith in Jesus" (Rom 3:26). In the cross, God both condemns evil and embraces sinners. The cross is why Exodus 23:7—where the Lord says, "I will not acquit the guilty"—and Romans 4:5—where Paul

17 M Volf, 'Christianity and Violence', in RS Hess and EA Martins (eds), *War in the Bible and Terrorism in the Twenty-first Century*, Eisenbrauns, 2008, p 12. Volf defines "absolute hospitality" as "a posture of welcoming the stranger without any preconditions". He expands: "'Absolute hospitality' seems generous and peaceful, until one remembers that unrepentant perpetrators and their unhealed victims would then have to sit around the same table and share a common home without adequate attention to the violation that has taken place."

says God “justifies the ungodly”—are both true.

This first objection also entails a false assumption—namely that forgiveness is costless. It is never costless. The idea that forgiveness is about simply ‘letting it go’ is a myth only believed by people who’ve never had to forgive anything significant. The truth is whenever we forgive someone, the cost of sin doesn’t just disappear; it is borne by the one offering the forgiveness.

Here’s a simple example: if you borrow $1000 from me and cannot repay it, I can choose to forgive you (to cancel the debt). But in the act of forgiveness, the $1000 doesn’t now magically appear in my bank account. If I forgive the debt, “forgiveness” is shorthand for “I will bear the cost”. Forgiveness is always like that. The cross, in this sense, is simply the inner logic of forgiveness writ large.

Is substitution just?

How can it be okay—morally, ethically, legally—for the innocent to be punished for the guilty?

At this point I freely concede that we can be our own worst enemies. We can present the substitution of Jesus in ways that create more problems than they solve.

Take, for example, the once-popular illustration of the railway controller who sees a train heading unstoppably for a crowded carriage, guaranteeing the death of all on board. The only hope is to divert the train to the other railway line. But in that moment the controller sees that his son, his beloved son, is playing on that other line. What can he do? He chooses to divert the train, thus killing his son but saving the lives of all the others.

As an illustration it gets an A+ for emotional impact, but (I'm afraid) a D– for theological accuracy. The whole thing, frankly, is a hot mess. As a picture of substitution, it places the son in the position of an innocent and unaware victim, and the father too is a hapless victim of circumstance. Now add to this picture of substitution the element of punishment, and the trouble only compounds.

So, let's say we move to a courtroom metaphor, with a judge offering to send his son to jail in place of a murderer. How is that in any way fair?

The problem, I submit, is in the simplistic nature of the metaphors. If God is a singular being, choosing random people to bear the punishment for other people's wrongs, we'd have a problem. Even if God is depicted as a human father choosing to punish his innocent but willing son, we're still not out of the woods. As Psalm 49:7 puts it "No one can redeem the life of another or give to God a ransom for them".

The real answer to the objection is to go into the heart of the trinitarian nature of God: "God was reconciling the world to himself in Christ" (2 Cor 5:19). Jesus, God the Son, was not a third party. In the trinitarian life of God, God was taking the weight of sin onto himself in the person of Jesus. The atonement is, in the phrase of John Stott, ultimately "the self-substitution of God".[18]

18 This is the title of chapter 6 of Stott's classic work *The Cross of Christ* (IVP, 1989).

Is penal substitution rational?

The objection here pushes us to stand back and ask: "What are we actually saying?" Are we really arguing that guilt and punishment are things that can be moved about from one person to another? What magical view of reality is this, where a random death on a cross two thousand years ago removes the guilt I incur for a sin I committed last Tuesday?

Fair questions.

My answer, for what it's worth, is to appeal to the limits of our language relative to the mystery of our subject, namely God. What I mean is this: Penal substitution is rational (it makes sense), but it is not rational*istic*. It does not (nor does it pretend to) dot every 'i' and cross every 't' in explaining the ways of God. We are talking about ultimate reality here. And to do so, we stretch human language to near breaking point. Sin has a penalty. Christ is our substitute. He brings our atonement. That much we can comprehend. But as to the precise 'mechanics' (and what an awful word to use in this context!) of how God achieves my forgiveness and reconciles the world to himself in Christ, what would I know!? As Wesley says in his great hymn 'And Can It Be', "Tis mystery all! The immortal dies!" And as Packer puts it in his classic essay:

> How was it possible for him to bear their penalty they do not claim to know, any more than they know how it was possible for him to be made man; but that he bore it is the certainty on which all their hopes rest.[19]

19 Packer, 'What did the cross achieve?'

Certainty that our sins are forgiven, and intellectual modesty about understanding precisely how—this is where penal substitutionary atonement places us. God promises that Jesus bore my sins on the cross. I take God at his word. I can trust him. It's a good place to be.

Good news for sinners

The doctrine of penal substitutionary atonement has caused headaches for the church's logicians. It's never caused much trouble for the church's poets. It may have fallen out of textbooks at key points, but it's never far from the church's hymnody; it's a truth perhaps better sung than said. The truth that Christ in his death took the penalty for our sins is something that fills our hearts even as it exercises our minds.

> My sin—oh, the bliss of this glorious thought!—
> My sin, not in part but the whole,
> Is nailed to the cross, and I bear it no more,
> Praise the Lord, praise the Lord, O my soul![20]

20 H Spafford, 'It Is Well With My Soul' [hymn], 1873.

Chapter 8
SILENCING GRANDMA
How the cross deals with our shame

Grandma and the lawyer

When your conscience speaks to you, what voice do you hear? Is it an inner lawyer, or an inner grandma?

This is the question of Australian missiologist David Williams.[21] In this metaphor, the inner lawyer is interested in right and wrong, good and evil, guilt and innocence. As you weigh your future options or consider your past actions, that inner lawyer will ask questions

21 D Williams, 'Introducing the pleasure-pain worldview', *The Gospel Coalition Australia*, 8 May 2018, accessed 16 February 2023 (au.thegospelcoalition.org/article/introducing-pain-pleasure-worldview).

such as "is it right or is it wrong?" He (I'm making this lawyer a man, mainly because my imagined inner lawyer looks and sounds exactly like Atticus Finch from *To Kill A Mockingbird*) is either your defence ("you were right!") or your prosecutor ("that was wrong!"). Either way, the inner lawyer deals in categories of guilt and innocence. He judges you and your actions according to fixed categories of right and wrong.

The inner grandma is different. She is not so much interested in guilt and innocence as in honour and shame. "What will people think?!" "You can't go out in that!" "How could you look them in the face again?" "Shame on you!"[22]

The inner lawyer is all about the evidence. Once the facts are in and the case is made, who cares what other people think? The inner grandma, on the other hand, is very much interested in what other people think. Indeed, that's how she's making her decisions. What will the neighbours think? Will this bring honour, or will it result in shame?

The cross and shame

The cross, which deals with our guilt, also deals with our shame. This is very good news. If no-one's ever told you about this before, allow me.

22 For the record, both of my grandmothers were lovely and not at all shamers. Yours probably were too. It's a metaphor.

Guilt and shame are related, but they are not identical experiences. Guilt is something you may or may not feel. It's possible to *be* guilty but not *feel* guilty, just as it's possible to feel guilty and not be guilty. A criminal may walk away from the courtroom with the objective status of 'guilty', but may personally feel defiant, numb, or even cheerful. Conversely, a tender-hearted person may experience feelings of guilt for things that were just mistakes, or for nothing at all. Our consciences are like faulty alarm systems, sometimes sounding off when there is nothing, and other times failing to alert us to a major problem.

Shame tends to be subjective. Shame is felt, and it is felt by our whole person. Guilt says, "I did the wrong thing"; shame says, "I am the wrong person". Guilt can focus on a specific event or action, while shame takes over our sense of who we are.

Guilt is personal. A young boy can kill a frog for fun, and then feel terrible about it. No-one needs to have seen it or objected to it. But shame is social. Shame has to do with our standing before others. To be humiliated or defiled before others is to be shamed. Even when shame is personal, we construct a little community out of ourselves and speak of ourselves in the third person: "I feel ashamed of my Self". A miserable little party of two: me, and the Self I am now heaping shame on.

The opposite of guilt is innocence; the opposite of shame is honour. And honour, like shame, is something bestowed on us by others.

Since the work of anthropologist Ruth Benedict (1887–1948), Western culture has commonly been understood as a guilt-innocence culture, while most non-Western cultures are seen as honour-shame cultures. The truth, of course, is more complex. But as a rough rule of thumb, this understanding holds up well enough—at least since the Enlightenment.[23] In the West, we tend to hear the inner lawyer. We are driven by an individual conscience. We seek innocence and avoid guilt. In other cultures, people are more likely to be driven by a communal voice, the voice channelled by grandma, calling us to seek honour and avoid shame.

Of course, non-Western cultures know guilt, just as Western culture knows shame. It's a matter of degrees. But for whatever reasons, in our culture the cross and shame haven't received the airtime they deserve. We have been underselling a key achievement of the cross. With the rise of social media, cancel culture and public shaming, grandma's back. And she's not happy. We need to know what the cross does to address our shame.

Thankfully, the Bible in general and the cross in particular have a lot to say about shame.

Shame in a fallen world and in the Bible

Shame, it should be noted, is not a universally condemned experience in Scripture. Shame, like guilt, can be a completely appropriate and useful response.[24]

23 For discussion, see GT Elshof, *For Shame: Rediscovering the virtues of a maligned emotion*, Zondervan, 2021.

24 Again, see Elshof's *For Shame* for a brilliant discussion of the positive uses of shame.

Shame gives the wider community a vote on my actions. To never feel shame is to be a sociopath. The person who is completely impervious to the judgement of the community is not generally someone you'd want running your country, teaching your children, or joining you for your summer holidays. Shame can be a good thing.

Or at least it's a good thing in a fallen world. In the garden, before the fall, "Adam and his wife were both naked, and they felt *no shame*" (Gen 2:25). They were not embarrassed or threatened. They anticipated no rejection or mockery or judgement from the one to whom they were exposed. Shame is only good in the way that locks on our doors or police on our streets are good. Shame (along with locks and police officers) was unknown in the garden, and will be retired from use in the new creation. It is a feature of the fall.

But while shame is useful in a fallen world, it has gone feral. Its ability to crush a soul, pillage joy, distort moral action and trap people under its crushing weight is horrifying. For every appropriate experience of shame, there are endless examples of Shame Gone Wild. Sexual abuse victims will feel shame for things that were manifestly not their fault. High-school students will be shamed for immutable characteristics, such as how they look or where they are from. Social *faux pas*, such as being seen with the 'wrong sort of people', can sink careers and harm lives.

In the Old Testament law, some forms of punishment were limited because to keep going would have meant "your fellow Israelite [would] be degraded in your eyes"

(Deut 25:3). Even where there was no question of the person's guilt, to add shame to their guilt was a bridge too far. It would have permanent social consequences.

Shame is embarrassing for both parties. It's embarrassing, of course, for the one shamed. But shame also catches the observer up in the experience. It is contagious. When Noah becomes drunk and lays naked and exposed, Shem and Japheth walk in backwards to cover their father's nakedness (Gen 9:23). The whole thing is shameful for Noah, but it's also shameful for his sons to have seen their father's indignity. The suffering servant of Isaiah 53 is "one from whom people hide their faces" (Isa 53:3). When we are ashamed, we want to run and hide. When we see the shamed, we want to turn our faces from them.

The shaming of Jesus

Jesus was never ashamed. But he was shamed. Deeply. Profoundly. He was not crushed by it. He crushed it.

If you look at the world through a guilt-and-innocence framework, it's possible to miss the emphasis on shame in the crucifixion of Jesus. But consider the event itself. Jesus was spat on and his head and face were struck (Matt 26:67, 27:30), his clothes were stripped off (Matt 27:28) and he was verbally mocked and insulted (Matt 27:29). None of these actions were in themselves physically painful. Being spat on doesn't hurt—it shames. Shame, rather than pain, is at the centre of the experience of the cross.

Jesus' life involved associating with people who threatened him with the social contagion of shame: a bleeding woman, tax collectors, prostitutes, Gentiles, and the like. These people were a threat to your social standing, to your place of honour within the community. Guilt is non-transferable; shame, on the other hand, is a highly transmissible disease.

In the case of Jesus, however, the contagion seemed to go the other way. Rather than those people bringing shame upon him, he bestowed honour upon them. The bleeding woman, for example, is healed and Jesus calls her "daughter"—she moved from shame to honour (Mark 5:25–34). Zacchaeus, a tax collector, is presented back to the community as a "son of Abraham" (Luke 19:9); the prodigal son in the story is presented back as the Father's son and the older brother's brother (Luke 15:21–32). In short, if you were associated with Jesus, the chances he'd move you from shame to honour were very high.

But in the crucifixion, this traffic moves in the opposite direction. Jesus, who moved so many from shame to honour, is himself moved from honour to shame. He is humiliated, embarrassed, degraded and shamed. Naked and defiled, he is abandoned by his friends. He becomes a threat to the honour of others. Take Peter's famous denial: association with Jesus is now a threat to Peter's social standing. "I never knew him" is the social equivalent of hand sanitizer, a surgical mask and a vaccine (see Luke 22:54–62). Jesus becomes the unvaccinated, unmasked carrier of a deadly social contagion.

How, then, does the cross deal with our shame? I want to offer three angles: Jesus exchanges our shame for honour; he experiences shame with us; and he pioneers the path to glory ahead of us.

Exchange: Jesus takes our shame and gives us honour

Jesus bore our shame for us. He took our shame and exchanged it for his honour. The logic of 2 Corinthians 5:21 applies here too: he who knew no shame became shamed for us, so that in him we might become the honoured ones of God.

Theologically, this is necessarily true. As the church fathers never tired of reminding us, Jesus' full incarnation as a human being was necessary for our salvation. "That which he has not assumed, he has not healed", as Gregory of Nazianzus put it.[25] Jesus came to reverse the curse of the fall. He did so by entering into that curse, by assuming to himself not just bits here and there, but all of it. If part of the curse is shame, we can be sure that Jesus entered into our shame.

What is a theological necessity is also an explicit teaching of Scripture. Notice, for example, the dynamics of sin and shame in these words from Hebrews:

25 Gregory of Nazianzus, 'Letters (Division 1): To Cledonius the Priest against Apollinarius', accessed 8 March 2023 (newadvent.org/fathers/3103a.htm).

> But we do see Jesus, who was made lower than the angels for a little while, now crowned with glory and honour because he suffered death, so that by the grace of God he might taste death for everyone.
>
> In bringing many sons and daughters to glory, it was fitting that God, for whom and through whom everything exists, should make the pioneer of their salvation perfect through what he suffered. Both the one who makes people holy and those who are made holy are of the same family. So Jesus is not ashamed to call them brothers and sisters. (Heb 2:9–11)

Guilt seeks forgiveness, but shame seeks acceptance. And that is precisely what God gives us in Christ.

Notice the logic: Jesus was honoured, yet "for a little while" he was made lower than the angels so he could taste death for everyone. He went through *shame*, and now he is not *ashamed* to call us his brothers and sisters. The gospel, which changes our legal status from guilty to innocent, also changes our social status from shamed to honoured, rejected to accepted. Through the work of the cross, Jesus (if I may put it this way) is proud of you.

With us: Jesus shares in our shame

Jesus also stands with us in the shame we receive on account of his name. Again, Hebrews:

> The high priest carries the blood of animals into the Most Holy Place as a sin offering, but the bodies are

> burned outside the camp. And so Jesus also suffered outside the city gate to make the people holy through his own blood. Let us, then, go to him outside the camp, bearing the disgrace he bore. (Heb 13:11–13)

Jesus suffered "outside the city gate". That is, his suffering included exclusion from the esteem of the community. He bore our disgrace to make us holy. But the encouragement is to "go to him outside the camp, bearing this disgrace he bore". What on earth can this mean?

For all of us some of the time, and for some of us most of the time, being a Christian has negative social consequences. We lose worldly honour. We become "foreigners and exiles" (1 Pet 2:11). Our social stocks diminish. Jesus has gone there too. He has experienced the shame of social exclusion more than any of us ever will. He has lost more social credits than we will ever have, let alone lose.

When are we called to 'bear disgrace' for the sake of Jesus? Where are we to go "outside the camp" with Jesus? Through association with his people.

In his parable of the sheep and the goats (Matt 25:31–46), Jesus asks us to envisage him as hungry, thirsty, a stranger, naked, sick or in prison—all states of contagious shame. But the people in the parable ask: when did we ever see *Jesus* in these situations? The answer is that whatever we did for "the least of these, brothers and sisters of mine", we did for Jesus (Matt 25:40). When we stand in solidarity with the people of God as they are being shamed, when we allow our social credit to diminish by refusing to disown them, we bear shame for the sake of Christ.

Think of the kid rejected at high school for their brave (if ham-fisted) stance for Jesus. Or the CEO who loses a board position because of their association with a local church. Or the teacher ostracized in a rural community for politely declining to wear a rainbow badge during Pride Month. In these situations, we have a choice: stand with our sister or brother and lose social credits, or distance ourselves from them and, in doing so, be ashamed of Jesus.

Trajectory: Jesus pioneers the path from shame to glory

Finally, when it comes to shame, Jesus pioneers the path for us. It's a path from shame to honour. And it's a path he invites us to follow.

The career of the son of God was V-shaped: from glory to shame and then back to (even greater) glory. Adam and Eve grasped for the fruit and were cast down. Jesus, although he was in very nature God, did not consider equality with God something to be grasped. He was obedient all the way down, even to death on a cross—and God lifted him up (Phil 2:5–11). The author of Hebrews encourages us to fix our eyes on Jesus, who is ...

> ... the pioneer and perfecter of faith. For the joy set before him he endured the cross, scorning its shame, and sat down at the right hand of the throne of God.

> Consider him who endured such opposition from sinners, so that you will not grow weary and lose heart. (Heb 12:2-3)

Jesus was able to endure the cross because of the joy set before him. What was he enduring? Specifically, the *shame* of the cross. And yet he was able to endure that shame in light of the joy ahead of him. Jesus didn't enjoy the shame (who does!?), but the glory and honour on the other side of shame kept him going.

In this, Jesus is our pioneer. Knowing that he went through shame to joy helps us to know the destination when we face similar trials. He mapped out the V-shaped path of the cross from shame to honour. We walk the way of the cross. "Whoever wants to be my disciple must deny themselves and take up their cross and follow me", says Jesus to the crowds (Mark 8:34). The apostle Peter makes a similar point:

> If you are insulted because of the name of Christ, you are blessed, for the Spirit of glory and of God rests on you. If you suffer, it should not be as a murderer or thief or any other kind of criminal, or even as a meddler. However, if you suffer as a Christian, do not be ashamed, but praise God that you bear that name. (1 Pet 4:14-16)

Suffering *as a Christian* (which Peter carefully disentangles from suffering for being a jerk) is in fact an honour, a glory to us, because we bear Christ's name. And that means we are on the same trajectory as him, awaiting the crown of glory (1 Pet 5:4), trusting that God's mighty hand will lift us up in due time (1 Pet 5:6).

Honour on the other side of shame

As author Gregg Ten Elshof argues, our culture is a paradox. We experience shame as entirely negative, but we see the strategy of shaming as powerful, useful and (thanks to social media) easily achievable. Shaming is everywhere. Grandma is back.

Shame can be useful. It can alert us to things that need to change. But only by the cross can we hear the words of honour on the other side of shame. Only through the death of Jesus can we now stand before God, knowing Jesus is not ashamed of us but honours us before the Father as his brothers and sisters.

Chapter 9

POWER AND LEADERSHIP

How the cross makes leaders servants and servants leaders

> Jews demand signs and Greeks look for wisdom, but we preach Christ crucified: a stumbling block to Jews and foolishness to Gentiles. (1 Cor 1:22–23)

A better way to lead

Leadership is getting people to go somewhere they wouldn't go themselves. Most leadership definitions are a variation of this theme. Whether it's Napoleon getting a huge army to move towards Moscow, a team leader getting the group to deliver financial reports by the end of the month, or a brave school student stopping an act of bullying, the leader gets people to where they wouldn't have gone themselves.

The question for leadership is, how? *How* will this group of people go to a place they wouldn't go themselves? Coercion, charisma, threat and reward will all do the trick. Jim Jones, the cult leader who moved his followers to South America, built a town and presided over a mass suicide, was nothing if not a leader. People went where they wouldn't have otherwise gone. But how? Through charisma, manipulation, coercion, reward, social pressure and violence.

Jim Jones is extreme. But in many less dramatic ways, we see poor leadership and ill-judged followership all around us. People who get people to go where they wouldn't go themselves, but do so through threat and flattery, fear and favour.

Jesus shows us a better way. He shows us through the cross.

Wisdom, power and a dead king

In the New Testament, the Corinthian church was being torn apart by a certain type of leadership. More accurately, it was being torn apart by a certain type of follower-ship. In our discussion of shame, we noted that shame is contagious. So is honour and prestige. By name-dropping the Right Sort of Leader as someone you follow, you can share in their glory. Assertions of social status and spiritual prestige can be acquired through which leader you are in contact with: "I follow Paul", "I follow Cephas", "I follow Apollos" (see 1 Cor 1:12). Ever noticed on Instagram how keen people are to be photographed with celebrity pastors? That's not a new thing. It goes all the way back to the New Testament. It's a case of toxic follower-ship, which is in turn a breeding ground for toxic leadership. For the antidote to this toxicity, Paul takes them back to the cross.

Then, as now, the church inherited some of its leadership ideals from the surrounding cultures. Paul highlights two sources for Corinth: Jewish and Greek.

The Jews, says Paul, looked for "signs". At the time of Jesus, Israel faced an emotionally and spiritually taxing reality. There was a huge and painful gap between what God had called them to be and what they could see with their eyes. And so the Jews of Judea looked for signs. Signs of power. Signs that God would do what he said he would do—flex his mighty arm, rescue them from their oppressors, and send the warrior-king, the Messiah, to establish the kingdom of God among them. After all, the original Messiah had been none other than David the giant slayer. Surely, a new Messiah would be at least as powerful; it stood to reason. The assumptions were understandable. But Paul offers a radically different way: "we preach Christ crucified" (1 Cor 1:23).

The word 'Christ' is from the Greek word meaning 'the anointed one'; 'Messiah' is from the Hebrew word with the same meaning. To say "we preach Christ crucified" to people expecting a warrior-rescuer is heard as a sheer contradiction. It is to say we preach Messiah Executed, Dead King, Crushed Crusher, Weakling Warrior.

Paul describes the message of the cross as "a stumbling block" (1 Cor 1:23). The concept is drawn from places such as Psalm 118 and Isaiah 28. The picture is of a building site. Stone, timber and tools have been delivered from all over the world. The construction workers have laid them out, each piece in keeping with the architect's vision and design. Like pieces of Ikea furniture just prior to assembly, each piece is separated out so that the builders can see how the parts relate to the whole.

But there's one piece that seems just not to fit. It looks so different from all the others—like it was made according to the wrong specifications. Perhaps it's intended for another project altogether, sent to this site through an administrative error at head office. And so it sits there, unused.

Eventually, it starts to get in the way. Builders stub their toes on it as they go about their work. It's fast becoming an occupational health and safety issue. The foreman asks, "Are we sure this piece is a mistake?"

"Yep", everyone agrees.

"Well, let's get it off the site, then." And so it is cast away.

But it turns out that what looked like a mistake was, in fact, the cornerstone of the whole edifice! It looked different, not because it was a mistake, but because it was the point of integration. It was the bit that brought everything else into shape.

> The stone the builders rejected
> has become the cornerstone. (Ps 118:22)

That's what the message of the cross is like for Paul. Strangely shaped. Odd-looking. Unsightly. Slightly off-message. But off he goes from town to town, synagogue to synagogue, with his message that Jesus of Nazareth is Messiah. The Messiah has come, and the day of God's kingdom has begun. But then, it is as if Paul takes the great stumbling block, this awkwardly large and weirdly shaped stone, and puts it between himself and his listener.

"Messiah crucified", he says.

"Oh", reply the puzzled crowd.

Wisdom and folly

Greek leadership ideals were different. Greek culture looked for strength, beauty and wisdom. Leadership prestige went to the one who could Keep Calm & Carry On. The ideal leader was the Philosopher-King who applied wisdom and order to the life of the disordered mass of humanity. Some 400 years before Jesus, Socrates had died at the hands of the Athenian rulers. But he philosophized on the way out, drinking the hemlock with composure, never losing his grip on reason. A 'compare-and-contrast' essay on the deaths of Jesus and Socrates would lean heavily on the contrast side. The death of Jesus would have meant a lot of things to a first-century Greek, but 'wise' would not have been one of them.

Christos Tsiolkas, in his bracing novel *Damascus* based on the life of the apostle Paul, captures well the strangeness and the scandal of the cross in the first-century world.

> My head ached. None of it made sense. I tried to understand. 'How did he die?'
>
> I waited. And I waited. Would no one answer?
>
> Paul's voice, for once, was deep and clear. "He was crucified by the Romans."
>
> And then I laughed. I laughed so hard I nearly fell off my stool. The old man attempted to fix my gaze once more with his serpent stare, but all I saw before me was a deluded and ridiculous old fool.[26]

These were the characteristic responses of Jews and Greeks to Paul's message: to Jews it looked weak; to Greeks, foolish.

For Paul, the cross was not an embarrassment. It was the power of God that brings salvation to everyone who believes (see Rom 1:16). And for that reason, it was also the secret to leadership. It contained within it the way to lead. And it was the way out of the tribal follower-ship which was then tearing the Corinthian church apart: "to those whom God has called, both Jews and Greeks, Christ the power of God and the wisdom of God" (1 Cor 1:24).

Worldly leadership so often creates the kind of dynamic that CS Lewis once referred to as "The Inner Ring". The idea is that we compete with one another by

26 C Tsiolkas, *Damascus*, Allen & Unwin, 2019, p 86.

accessing circles (or "rings") that have more and more proximity to the leader or people of influence. We look at others who seem to have the ear of the leaders and access to the inner circle. Jealous, we either seek to break into that circle, or form other circles which we then use as status symbols over the others. Leaders may use their followers, but followers also use their leaders. We project onto them our own ideals, and we seek from them some status we can leverage over others. A Christian community that acquiesces to these dynamics signs up for misery and dysfunction. Those who have the attributes favoured in the wider culture win; those who don't, lose. The church becomes just another place in which the psychodrama of worldly leadership expectations gets played out.

The cross plays into no-one's expectations. It offers no home-ground advantage. Not to Jew, nor Greek. Nor secular people. Nor religious people. Nor good people. Nor bad people. No-one. It creates its own landing space. And it forces each of us to put aside whatever natural advantages or disadvantages we might have, and to stand somewhere new.

Paul's weakness

Understanding the cross happens as we listen to the Scriptures and learn to see the cross differently. It is to crack the puzzle, solve the riddle, and see that the power and wisdom of God is found in the most unlikely of all places. And once we see it differently, we see all things differently.

In the case of Paul, it changed not only the message, but the method of the messenger:

> And so it was with me, brothers and sisters. When I came to you, I did not come with eloquence or human wisdom as I proclaimed to you the testimony about God. For I resolved to know nothing while I was with you except Jesus Christ and him crucified. I came to you in weakness with great fear and trembling. My message and my preaching were not with wise and persuasive words, but with a demonstration of the Spirit's power, so that your faith might not rest on human wisdom, but on God's power. (1 Cor 2:1–5)

For many today, discovering the cross has entailed a move from being secular to being, in some sense, religious. But prior to his conversion, a lack of religiosity was not Paul's problem. He had been a religious zealot—which in modern English means something like 'really into religion', but for Paul meant something more specific. It was that branch of religion that saw violence as necessary to defend and promote religious causes. Our word for that is 'terrorism'. And terrorism is a time-honoured method of getting people to go somewhere they wouldn't go themselves. It's amazing what you can get people to do when they're terrified.

The message of the cross changed all that for Paul. It *had* to change all that for Paul. If Christ crucified was God's power and wisdom, religious terrorism must necessarily be its opposite. Paul's *modus operandi* had to change completely. No longer could violence in the name of religion be justified. God was winning the world, not through the perpetrators of violence, but through one of its victims.

The cross and cultural context

This new outlook also changed the way Paul thought about contextualizing the message. The cross subverts all the world's cultures, including Western culture. We sometimes don't notice this, in the way that fish don't notice water. Imagine you are in a church that supports some missionaries in, say, Bali. You receive their latest prayer letter, full of all the normal sort of missionary fare—reports on the evangelistic contacts, the support levels, the kids. But then you notice something:

> In our efforts to connect with local people, we've recently discovered that by going to temple, lighting incense, and saying a little prayer to one of the Hindu gods, we've won a much greater acceptance. It has really relieved the tension we've felt for years.

Wait, what!? It's time to get the missions committee together for an urgent discussion.

But now, imagine you're a missionary in a Western context. Writing to your sending church, you report:

> In our efforts to connect with local Westerners, we've recently discovered that by assertive managerial

> leadership, celebrity endorsement, a quest for self-actualization and a more relaxed attitude to sexuality, we've won a much greater acceptance. It has really relieved the tension we've felt for years.

Wait, what?!

Paul goes to Corinth, a Greek city, and says: "My message and my preaching were not with wise and persuasive words" (1 Cor 2:4). That looks like a mission fail of the first order, a missed opportunity to contextualize the message. If any one group was going to appreciate wise and persuasive words, it was the Greeks.

Paul was more than capable of using both wise and persuasive words (indeed, he is ironically demonstrating those very capacities in this chapter), and in the city of Corinth he would have found an enthusiastic audience. But Paul put that aside, and he did so on purpose. Why? *Because what you win them with is what you win them to*. Paul wants to win them *to* the cross, so he wins them *with* the cross: "For I resolved to know nothing while I was with you except Jesus Christ and him crucified" (1 Cor 2:2).

Paul does not mean, "I only ever gave sermons on penal substitutionary atonement". No doubt he taught regularly on all kinds of subjects and proclaimed to them "the whole will of God" (Acts 20:27). But the statement here is about the *kind* of Christ he preached. He says in effect: "The only Christ you were ever going to hear about on my lips was the one that was crucified".

The cross today: True power and true wisdom

The cross continues to be a stumbling block, both inside and outside religious communities.

On the one hand, the doctrine of the cross is under enormous pressure in the church today as people reject the idea of the cross as a penalty and Christ's death as a substitute. Mocked as a form of divine child abuse, rejected as extreme and insane, as a myth of redemptive violence. Seen as offensive to human dignity because, well, we can't have been *that* bad. The theologian H Richard Niebuhr rightly denounced a situation in which "a God without wrath brought men without sin into a kingdom without judgment through the ministrations of a Christ without a cross".[27]

But there is another risk—the risk not of a cross without judgement, but of a cross without reach. The risk is that our grasp of the cross will be technically true, but tiny. In the Bible, the cross is big. It should be big among us. And if it is big among us, it will shape the way we lead and the way we follow.

The cross is both the subversion *and* the fulfilment of all our leadership longings. The truth is, leadership (like work and marriage) is part of God's original created order. The reason there's a bunch of actionable wisdom in secular leadership books is that those books (the good ones, at least) are based on observations of the world

27 HR Niebuhr, *The Kingdom of God in America*, Wesleyan University Press, 1988, p 193.

God made. They are tethered to the created order.

The cross introduces a subversive dynamic (*servant* leadership), but it also preserves the dynamic of the created order (servant *leadership*). The cross subverts, but it doesn't say up is down, left is right, and people will be moved forward by you standing still and inviting them to walk over you. Leadership is the job, and it involves all sorts of competencies you could learn through an MBA, or a leadership intensive, or a bunch of good books. You can learn to be a better leader. And you can learn good things from secular books. Check for babies before you dispose of that bathwater.

'Servant' is the cross-shaped method, the attitude of the heart of someone who's been won by the cross to see that a life given for God and for others is the life of true and lasting value.

Paul wanted to undermine the Corinthians' quest for power, their pretensions to wisdom. He wanted to allow the cross to do its crushing work on human arrogance and pretension. No flattery here, and certainly no boasting: "God chose the lowly things of this world and the despised things—and the things that are not—to nullify the things that are, so that no one may boast before him" (1 Cor 1:28–29). Boastful, attention-seeking leadership is out of tune with the note struck by the cross.

But notice: "You are in Christ Jesus, who has become for us wisdom from God—that is, our righteousness, holiness and redemption (1 Cor 1:30). The cross both subverts and fulfils. It refuses to flatter our vanities or leave our idols un-toppled. And yet Christ is the power and the wisdom of God. Christ and his cross are, in some deeper and fuller sense, precisely what we are looking for. Our stunted, wicked ways are also expressions of longings and desires which are rightly met in the strange place of the cross. In other words, the cross not only nullifies our quest for power; it shows us true power. It not only frustrates our quest for wisdom; it shows us true wisdom.

Leading (and following) in the shadow of the cross

So, how do we lead in the shadow of the cross? Leadership is still a thing. Nations, businesses, communities, families and churches all need to be led, and the cross doesn't collapse leadership into a timid negotiation of keeping everyone happy at any cost. We can do good things in the world when we lead people to where they wouldn't otherwise have gone.

On any definition, Jesus is the ultimate leader. We were headed for hell, but Jesus brings us to God—talk about bringing people where they wouldn't have otherwise gone! And yet Jesus, the ultimate leader, did not leave us with a model of power-hungry, push-and-shove leadership. His leadership was a *servant* leadership. But it was still *leadership*. The kingdom community is not a leadership-free environment. Good leadership is still possible among the people of God. But good leadership is shaped by the way of the cross:

> "You know that those who are regarded as rulers of the Gentiles lord it over them, and their high officials exercise authority over them. Not so with you. Instead, whoever wants to become great among you must be your servant, and whoever wants to be first must be slave of all. For even the Son of Man did not come to be served, but to serve, and to give his life as a ransom for many." (Mark 10:42-45)

And for followers (most of us most of the time), Paul's counsel is surprisingly ecstatic:

> So then, no more boasting about human leaders! All things are yours, whether Paul or Apollos or Cephas or the world or life or death or the present or the future—all are yours, and you are of Christ, and Christ is of God. (1 Cor 3:21–23)

Paul says, in effect, "Don't rip yourself off—in Christ, you get it all!" He doesn't collapse Paul, Apollos and Cephas into anonymous service deliverers. Like all leaders, they bring different things to the table. Extroversion or introversion. Different insights. Different personalities. Different gifts. In Christ, they have all been given to us. Therefore, says Paul, drink it all in! Paul's brilliance, Augustine's searching insights, Calvin's orderly thought, Luther's energy, Bonhoeffer's bravery, Corrie Ten Boom's piety, GK Chesterton's exuberance, and so on. It's all yours!

This approach to follower-ship undermines broken models of leadership. In the shadow of the cross, we no longer need to compete with one another on the basis of our access to power, our association with those leaders currently in favour.

And when we lead, what are we? "Only servants, through whom you came to believe—as the Lord has assigned to each his task" (1 Cor 3:5). Leaders are servants, assigned with a task, given a role. If you are in leadership, you are an expression of God's kindness to those you lead. You have been given to them, not to build a cult of personality or develop your own sense of self-validation. You are a servant. Your service is leadership. Work hard. Move God's people faithfully and determinedly to the good places they wouldn't have otherwise gone. Learn your craft. Give it all you've got. And rest in the freedom of knowing all you've got is not all they need.

Chapter 10

A USER'S GUIDE TO THE LORD'S SUPPER

What's going on at the Supper?

"We are what we repeatedly do." So says Aristotle.[28] Christians have a suite of practices that we repeatedly do—read our Bibles, pray, gather with God's people—because we believe that, over time, these practices will form and re-form us. And almost all churches celebrate a meal variously called 'the Lord's Supper', 'Holy Communion' or

28 Or at least, so the internet misattributes to Aristotle. While a reasonable summary of Aristotle's views, the quote seems to have come from an English author called Will Durant (attempting to capture some of Aristotle's thought) in 1926.

‘the Eucharist’.[29] It is one of those things we repeatedly do. And we do so specifically to remember Jesus’ death.

My purpose in this short chapter is not to give a complete account of everything the Lord’s Supper may or may not mean. Nor will I look to arbitrate between what different church leaders and traditions have claimed about the Supper. I have in mind the normal church member who will clock up a fair few Lord’s Suppers before they shuffle off this mortal coil. What are some tools we can use to understand what’s going on? I have three: Covenant renewal, participation in the death of Jesus, and proclamation of that same death. That should be enough to keep us going!

Covenant renewal

Historically, the big questions around the Lord’s Supper have been on the nature of the food and drink itself. Is the bread *really* the body of Jesus? Is the wine *really* his blood? If not, then what does it mean to say, “This is my body”? Is it spiritual language? Symbolic language? A mere aid to memory?

29 A word of clarification. In these discussions, “the Last Supper” refers to the meal Jesus shared with his disciples on the night before he died, while “the Lord’s Supper” is the meal Christians share in his memory. We discussed the Last Supper in chapter 1, so here we’re thinking about the Lord’s Supper we share. And, of course, the latter is based on the former.

I think we are asking the wrong question. A raw choice between 'real' or 'symbolic' is a little like asking of a wedding ring, "Is this ring the actual marriage, or just a meaningless piece of gold?" It's a textbook case of the law of the excluded middle, the logical fallacy which presents two extreme options as if they are the only two. In the case of options for the significance of the Lord's Supper, we are entitled, with Oliver Twist, to assert, "Please, sir, I want some more".

Consider the wedding ring. It is, obviously, not a marriage. That's absurd. But, in the context of the wedding service, neither is it *just* a circle of gold. We need a third option. It is a *sign* of the covenant made between the husband and wife. It is, in that context, highly significant.

The language of "covenant" is not used a lot in the New Testament, but Jesus uses it at the Last Supper. And that is significant. I believe that, as Christians participate in the Lord's Supper, the best way to understand it is as a covenant renewal ceremony. It's not a covenant ceremony—that covenant was made once for all on the cross in the body and blood of Christ. But neither it is *merely* a memory aid or a convenient visual symbol of the death of Jesus, a way of reaching out to those who are visual learners. If it is a covenant renewal ceremony, it is not simply something to watch, but something to participate in.

Participation in Jesus' death

It is not possible to have the Lord's Supper alone—a fact worth reflecting on. Many other aspects of Christian devotion, such as prayer, Bible reading, singing and fasting, can happen alone. In some cases (such as prayer), solitude brings certain advantages. But not the Lord's Supper. It is necessarily a shared meal, an activity requiring two or more players. This points to important vertical and horizontal truths.

The *vertical* truth is that the Lord's Supper includes us in Jesus' death as participants, not simply observers. Historically, Jesus died very much alone—a point to which the Gospels regularly draw attention. He died instead of us and for us. But the first disciples were invited, ahead of that lonely death, to claim their stake in what was about to happen. The death of Jesus and its benefits are not things that happen outside of us, to which we merely assent. As the apostle Paul will go on to write, we were baptized into his death (see Rom 6:3–4). We died *with* Christ (see Rom 6:6; Gal 2:20). We died *in* him. This doctrine of our union with Christ was taught by Jesus himself, through the Lord's Supper, before it was taught by Paul.

The *horizontal* truth is that what's true for me is true for the people with whom I share the meal. We are all in this together. We are constituted as a new people by Jesus' death. In the Lord's Supper, we reaffirm our common identity and fellowship with those who are at the table with us.

Some aspects of the Lord's Supper are incidental—what reformed theology sometimes calls the 'circumstances'. The grain used for the bread, the precise vintage of the wine, the bakery or vineyard employed and the building in which it takes place—these are all incidental 'circumstances' of the Supper. Just as we are liable to pour meaning into 'circumstances' (such as claiming the breaking of the bread symbolizes Jesus' broken body), our modern celebrations of the Supper are sometimes prone to miss elements that are important to the meal's meaning. For example, sharing from one loaf and drinking from one cup are both significant in the Bible. "Drink from it, all of you", says Jesus (Matt 26:27). "We all share the one loaf", says Paul (1 Cor 10:17). Using one loaf and one cup presents both logistical and hygienic challenges. I'm not arguing against individual cups or using more than one loaf. But it is worth noting that, in the New Testament, these are features of what the meal means and how that meaning is derived.

Paul chastises the church in Corinth because in their celebration of the Supper they do not discern "the body of Christ" (1 Cor 11:29). This is not a failure to perceive that the bread *is* the body of Christ, but rather a failure to perceive that the *community* with whom they share it is the body of Christ. It is their failure to recognize Christ in each other rather than Christ in the bread. Their sin was to have the audacity to divide into rich and poor, in-group and out-group, haughty and hungry, and still have the temerity to describe what they were doing as "the Lord's Supper". No! The cross binds us simultaneously to Christ and to each other. It may well be appropriate at the Lord's table to close our eyes to examine ourselves and confess our sins. But it is also appropriate to open our eyes, look around that room of people and say: "These are also people for whom Christ died. This is the body of Christ. Am I, in my heart and life, in the way I treat these people, discerning in them the body of Christ?"

Proclamation of his death

The Lord's Supper is (I hope it hardly needs saying) no place for party politics. But politics understood more broadly is about the question of power and authority. The central Christian claim is that "Jesus is Lord". It's a straightforwardly political claim. It's about who has authority. Not just in my heart, or even in the church, but in the whole universe.

The Lord's Supper is a proclamation of the gospel. The Passover was also political. It was about a people escaping a tyrant under the mighty hand of God. And when you continued to celebrate it under the nose of the Roman forces, it couldn't help but continue to take on a political hue. In the Lord's Supper, says Paul, we "proclaim the Lord's death until he comes" (1 Cor 11:26). Proclaim it to whom? To each other? Yep, sure. To the unbeliever perhaps present at church? Probably. But I put it to you that we also proclaim the Lord's death to the powers of darkness, to the principalities of this world, to Satan, and to the gates of hell. As we'll explore in the next chapter, the cross is the means of God's emphatic defeat of the demonic realm. Through the church, God is making his manifold wisdom known to the rulers and authorities (see Eph 3:10). And when we come together at the Lord's table, we manifest ourselves as the people brought together through the death of Jesus. The powers of darkness don't like this. They like disorder, alienation, enmity. When we come together at the Lord's table, we remind them that the cross is how God is reconciling the universe to himself (see 2 Cor 5:19). That the forces of evil have been defeated. The Lord's Supper might involve handshakes and kisses, but it is, in its own quiet way, a fist in the air. It is a sign and warning signal to the forces of evil that Jesus has conquered; that sin, death and Satan are on notice. The game is up. Jesus is Lord. And every knee is on track to one day bow before him.

Does the cross then, speak to politics, to nation states, to rulers and authorities? Yes! How could it not? The cross is how God reclaims the rule of the world for himself. It is the way through which earthly rulers and authorities lay down their crowns before the King of kings (Ps 2:10–12, Rev 4:10). This is not the same thing as to say that the church should have authority over the state, or even that the church should be confused with the state. Nor should Christians conflate national allegiance with allegiance to Christ or seek to control the apparatus of the state via its overthrow.

The way of the cross is more subtle, and its influence more powerful in the long term. It is brought about as men and women come under the influence of the cross, and by it begin to see the way of true power and true wisdom differently, and then apply that to the areas in which they serve, including government. Take, for example, William Wilberforce (1759–1833), who led the movement for the abolition of slavery in the British Empire. He didn't do so by mounting a secular argument, nor by leaving his religious convictions at the door as he went into parliament. Rather, he allowed the logic of the cross to extend to the dignity of the victims of slavery. We strike a political point every time we sing the words of the Christmas Carol 'O Holy Night':

> Truly he taught us to love one another,
> His law is love, and his gospel is peace.
> Chains he shall break, for the slave is our brother,
> And in his name all oppression shall cease.
> Sweet hymns of joy in grateful chorus raise we,
> Let all within us praise his holy name.
> Christ is the Lord! Then ever, ever praise we!
> His power and glory evermore proclaim![30]

His power and glory will continue to break chains and will, eventually, end all oppression. He will do it through the power and glory of the cross. When we share in the Lord's Supper, we proclaim the power and glory of the cross to each other and the world.

30 A Adam, 'O Holy Night' [hymn], 1847.

Chapter 11

HOW TO USE THE CROSS IN THE EVENT OF A ZOMBIE APOCALYPSE

Entering the battlefield

What is the problem to which the cross is the solution? Different biblical pictures suggest different answers. In the law court, the cross is answering a justice problem. In the slave market, it's a freedom problem. In the language of personal relationships, it's a work of reconciliation. But one of the contexts in which the New Testament encourages us to understand the cross is a battlefield. Not just a standard issue, nation-versus-nation battlefield, but an all-out Zombie Apocalypse. The cross, says the New Testament, comes into *that* context and, through a masterstroke of subterfuge, double-crossing and military genius, wins the war and leaves the enemy dazed, confused and defeated. This chapter is about that victory. It's about how the cross won the Zombie Apocalypse.

Focus

It might be worth clarifying that the New Testament does not predict a literal apocalyptic battle between humans and zombies. But it most certainly speaks in battle language. And it's a theme we sometimes miss. There's a famous experiment in which people are told to look carefully at basketball players and count how many times the players in white shirts pass the ball to each other.[31] What around half of all participants don't notice is that, right in the middle of the video, a person in a gorilla suit walks into the middle of the shot, dances, and then walks off. Once you've seen it, you can't miss it. But it's easy to miss if your focus is elsewhere. Such is the case when modern Western people read the Bible and fail to see the spiritual forces it speaks about. They are everywhere, hidden in plain sight. If you read the Bible with Western lenses, you're not expecting to find them, and so you don't.

The Bible pictures the world as a war zone. It's the

31 It's called the "selective attention test", if you want to look it up on YouTube: DJ Simons and C Chabris, 'Selective attention test' [video], *Daniel Simons*, YouTube, 11 March 2010, accessed 17 February 2023 (youtu.be/vJG698U2Mvo).

site of a cosmic battle, a spiritual conflict of epic proportions, complete with spies, propaganda, counter-insurgencies, casualties and clashes. And the cross is the counterintuitive masterstroke in God's defeat of the satanic forces. The language is militaristic. It's about winning a battle. And this is not a marginal theme on the edge of Scripture. It's right there in the centre of the story, like the gorilla on the basketball court. We just need the eyes to see it.

Just like the gorilla, once you've seen it, you can't unsee it. But for our purposes, let's have a look at a passage where the whole theme is so front, centre and in-your-face that missing it would be quite a feat. It's in Paul's letter to the church in Colossae.

> See to it that no one takes you captive through hollow and deceptive philosophy, which depends on human tradition and the elemental spiritual forces of this world rather than on Christ.
>
> For in Christ all the fullness of the Deity lives in bodily form, and in Christ you have been brought to fullness. He is the head over every power and authority. In him you were also circumcised with a circumcision not performed by human hands. Your whole self ruled by the flesh was put off when you were circumcised by Christ, having been buried with him in baptism, in which you were also raised with him through your faith in the working of God, who raised him from the dead.
>
> When you were dead in your sins and in the uncircumcision of your flesh, God made you alive with

> Christ. He forgave us all our sins, having cancelled the charge of our legal indebtedness, which stood against us and condemned us; he has taken it away, nailing it to the cross. And having disarmed the powers and authorities, he made a public spectacle of them, triumphing over them by the cross. (Col 2:8–15)

Notice the language: Don't get 'taken captive', beware of the "spiritual forces"; "powers and authorities" are now "disarmed" and "made a public spectacle of". This is a war zone. And in that war zone, an unambiguous, decisive victory over the enemy has taken place. And the victory has been won through—of all things—a crucifixion. How does *that* work?

Let's break it down into three elements: the enemy; the tactical move; and the outcome.

The enemy

In his classic, ancient guide to warfare, *The Art of War*, Sun Tzu advises the would-be warrior to know both themselves and their enemy.

> If you know the enemy and know yourself, you need not fear the result of a hundred battles. If you know yourself but not the enemy, for every victory gained you will also suffer a defeat. If you know neither the enemy nor yourself, you will succumb in every battle.[32]

32 Sun Tzu, *The Art of War* (L Giles trans), Dover Publications, 2002, p 51.

Let's go with that. Who, then, is our enemy?

At one level, 'the enemy' in Colossae are the all-too-human teachers who are threatening to take the Christians captive through "hollow and deceptive philosophy" (v 8). Here is an enemy you can see. They would have had names, personalities and followers. Once you have identified who they are and worked out that their philosophy is an entrapment, the threat is clear. So too is the solution: stop listening to false teaching. Remove the invitation to next year's Youth Convention. And teach the truth.

But this enemy, it turns out, is more complicated. Behind the more observable threat of false teaching lie "the elemental spiritual forces" (v 8), and the "powers and authorities" of verses 10 and 15. Who are these guys?

The *stoicheia* (the Greek word behind "elemental spiritual forces") are the evil spiritual beings who work against the purposes of God in our world. Together with the "powers and authorities" and the demons of the Gospels, these constitute an army of the undead.

I can get a little more specific, but not much. The challenge here is that these unseen and malevolent forces are frequently 'in shot' (to use a film metaphor), but rarely do they occupy centre stage (to switch, mid-sentence, from film to theatre). What we know about them must be pieced together from a series of disparate lines of evidence, like crooks caught in grainy CCTV footage. With that caveat in mind, here we go.

God is the Creator of all that is, seen and unseen. In the unseen realm, God created his heavenly host of angels.

The angels are older than us. They were God's

heavenly council, his entourage, his courtly servants. But, just as there was a rebellion on earth led by Adam and Eve (Genesis 3), it seems there was a rebellion in heaven. Satan and his angels rebelled against their role, just as we rebelled against ours. This heavenly rebellion is never front-and-centre, but there are hints, inferences and pieces of the puzzle throughout Scripture. Angels were present, and were busily rejoicing, when God created the physical universe (Job 38:4-7). And then who are the "gods" in the "great assembly" of Psalm 82? Who are the sons of God in Deuteronomy 32:8?[33] Where did the serpent come from in Genesis 3, and why is he already God's enemy? Who is the "morning star" who has fallen from heaven and been cast down to the earth in Isaiah 14:12? Put these and other passages together and a picture emerges: just as World War II was a war fought in two main theatres (Europe and the Pacific), so the war between good and evil has ever been fought on two fronts: in both the seen and the unseen realms.[34]

Now, this is where the CCTV footage gets a little grainier. In the Gospels there are "demons" (sometimes translated as "impure spirits" or "unclean spirits"). These may well be those fallen angels. But they may also be the spirits of the dead—that is, ghosts. And, who knows, perhaps there are other unseen spirits who are

33 See the NIV footnote for Deuteronomy 32:8.

34 For a detailed and compelling account, see M Heiser, *The Unseen Realm: Recovering the Supernatural Worldview of the Bible* (Lexham Press, 2015).

neither fallen angels nor ghosts. The Bible doesn't provide a definitive list of these things. Whatever or whoever is there, two things will be true about them: first, they are God's creatures, and second, they have been co-opted into the rebellion of the unseen.

One more thing: unlike World War II, in which the European and Pacific theatres were really rather separate, in this war the seen and unseen realms are much more integrated. Both are absolutely part of the one great War between God and evil. They are not hermetically sealed off from each other. Indeed, they mirror one another. Characters from one realm regularly appear in the other. And events in our world are often not easily disentangled from events in the other. It's not possible to say definitively that one battle was 'spiritual' and another was 'human'. And nowhere is this truer than in the case of the cross.

The tactical move and its outcome

In the Bible's unfolding story, the cross is the point at which a decisive victory against the enemy is won. But how? That's what Paul parses out for us in Colossians.

On the cross our sins are paid for and forgiven. This much is familiar territory. But notice what Paul says: In cancelling "the charge of our legal indebtedness", Jesus also "disarmed the powers and authorities" (Col 2:14-15). The logic, I believe, is that he took away from them the thing that gave them their power—namely, our sin and guilt.

The name 'Satan' means 'accuser'. It's less a name and more a job title. The work of Satan is to accuse the saints day and night. And there's a problem here: he has a point. We really did have a charge against us. It really did condemn us. But Jesus, in his death, took that away. He nailed it to the cross. And by doing so, he took from our spiritual enemies all of their live ammunition. After the cross, they are still attacking. But now they're firing blanks. They have been disarmed.

This, in other words, is the New Testament's Zombie Apocalypse. It is a marshalling of the satanic forces, the evil agents of the unseen realm, against the Lord and against his anointed one.

Notice *when* it's happening, by the way. We are accustomed to thinking the great battle with evil is ahead of us, that the Zombie Apocalypse is the dark prophecy of what lies in our world's future. But here, the apocalypse was at the cross. The great battle is behind us, not in front of us. The forces of evil are not now marshalling their troops for a future encounter at which they'll give it all they've got. They've already given it all they had, and it did not go well for them. It was a colossal blunder, an own goal, an embarrassing defeat. They were routed, outsmarted, trumped. The Accuser's accusations no longer stick (see Rom 8:33–34). The logic of guilt and shame have been undone by the cross. The "strong man" is bound (Mark 3:27) and now forces of light are robbing his house.

Part of the deliciousness of this victory was that, in one sense, the forces of darkness had no choice but to kill the Messiah. Haters gotta hate. You send the Son of God to earth, and the powers of darkness essentially had no choice but to kill him. And yet, in nailing him to the cross, they effectively disarmed themselves and sealed their own fate. The human actors, such as Herod and Pontius Pilate, conspired against God's holy servant. But in doing so, "they did what [God's] power and will had decided beforehand should happen" (Acts 4:28). And their unseen counterparts did the same. At precisely the point of the world's greatest manifestation of evil (killing the Son of God), they sealed the fate of evil. And if evil at its most evil accidentally undoes evil, then evil won't win. It couldn't win, even when everyone thought it was winning. At the cross, the forces of evil are revealed to be gormless, pathetic losers. This is good news.

And what is the outcome? The win is so decisive that Paul pictures the celebration as a kind of Roman victory parade. Back in the day, after a major military victory, the Romans would host a victory march through the streets of Rome. Out front you'd have the generals, then the soldiers, all receiving the praise of the crowd. And then, behind them all were the captives. These prisoners of war would be led behind the procession—disarmed, humiliated and mocked. These were warriors who, maybe only a week ago, presented a clear and present threat to the safety of Rome. But there they now were, dragged along in chains, harmless and helpless. A public spectacle at the mercy of the crowd. Triumphed over by the might of Rome.

Look again at Colossians 2:15: "And having disarmed

the powers and authorities, he made a public spectacle of them, triumphing over them by the cross". Do you see!? In his death, Jesus disarmed the powers and authorities. He undid the elemental spiritual forces of the world. They are now paraded before us, humiliated and pathetic, objects of ridicule.

"Be not afraid"

The victory of Jesus over the powers and principalities of the unseen realm is not just a biblical curiosity. For many people, it is one of the most treasured and practical achievements of the cross.

For several years, I was involved in a preachers' training program in the Solomon Islands. The program was excellent and my teaching serviceable, and over the years progress was made.

One evening, on the last night of the program, a bunch of us were chatting, singing and eating. Having been the teacher during the week, I now faded into the background as others led the conversation. One of the pastors suggested we all pray for each other before heading to bed and home the next day.

The first man shared that he was worried a witch-doctor was targeting his daughter. Another prayed for courage to tell his ageing parents he didn't want to be involved in some of the village ceremonies that invoked spirits. And another, though a Christian pastor, confessed he still feared his totem animal (a crocodile) was angry with him for abandoning the ancestral religion.

These are not the fears a pastor working in a Western context often hears. But in voicing them, these brothers and sisters spoke for millions across the world. And they spoke of the fears that shaped the world into which the message of the cross first came. The message of the cross doesn't belittle these fears or those who hold them. It declares victory over them! It tells them, "Be not afraid". The enemy has been overcome. The enemy has been humiliated by the cross.

One song regularly sung in churches captures the dynamic of this victory well.

> When Satan tempts me to despair,
> and tells me of the guilt within,
> upward I look, and see him there,
> who made an end of all my sin.[35]

The whole Satanic-guilt-religious industrial complex has been undone from the inside out. Sin and guilt—Satan's power source—have been dealt with. The enemy has been thwarted and shamed. And we live our lives in the wake of that victory. Good news, indeed.

35 C Bancroft, 'Before the Throne of God Above' [hymn], 1863.

Chapter 12

THE CROSS AND WHAT WE DO IN CHURCH

Regulative or normative?

Imagine for a moment that you were given free rein over all the things that happen at your church in a Sunday service: the music, the prayers, the Bible readings, the preaching, the Lord's Supper—everything we might think of under the umbrella of 'worship'.[36] What would

36 The Bible doesn't have a single word that captures what we mean in English by 'worship'—that is, those specific activities (such as prayer and singing) by which we express reverence and devotion to God. And, as I will argue later in this chapter, when the New Testament applies Old Testament worship language, it is usually to all of life rather than to specific activities (see, for example, Rom 12:1–2). I use the word 'worship' here in its normal English sense, without meaning to flatten the rich vocabulary or biblical-theological unfolding of the related concepts in Scripture.

you do? What changes, if any, would you make?

Think about the music. Too many hymns? More contemporary? More psalms? Perhaps *only* psalms? Or how about the practice of the Lord's Supper? Too frequent? Not frequent enough? Should the bread be leavened or unleavened? Wine or grape juice? Sombre or celebratory?

Consider what changes you would make, and ask yourself: Why? What are the limits on what should happen in church? When do we have freedom? Where has the word of God already made the decision for us? Who gets to decide what we may do, what we must do, and what we must not do in church? And can the cross help us to find a way forward?

In asking these questions, we've jumped into the middle of a significant debate, sometimes framed as the 'regulative principle' versus the 'normative principle' of worship. Simply put, when it comes to the question of what we may do in our church services, the regulative principle says we should only do that which God's word expressly commands; the normative principle says we should avoid what God's word expressly forbids, but otherwise we have the freedom to run our church gatherings in whatever way we think is most beneficial.

As one modern example, the Anglican Church, with its tradition of common prayer and orderly worship, is an expression of the normative principle. Anglicanism is essentially reformed Catholicism; its practices come from a process of sifting through the forms of the pre-Reformation church, removing what was contrary to

God's word, and keeping the elements that it deemed helpful, even if there wasn't a specific verse for them. Traditional Pentecostalism, on the other hand, reflects a kind of regulative principle: it takes the references to tongues and prophecy from Bible passages such as 1 Corinthians 14 and Acts 2 as an indication of what ought to happen in every church today, not merely as a description of what once happened in a church.

'Regulative versus normative' is a complex debate, but fortunately we don't need to wade into the depths of it here. Our interest is simply in whether the cross helps to guide our thinking about the big principles. I'm convinced that it does.

Let's begin by turning to the Old Testament—specifically, to our previous study of Leviticus, which is going to help us lay the groundwork for answering the questions posed above.

Adam, Israel and Levitical priests

The Levitical priests were the worship leaders of the Old Testament in that it was their job to guide, guard and protect the holy worship of the holy God. They were not, for example, allowed to drink on the job. That's probably a good idea all the time, but here the reason is specific: "so that you can distinguish between the holy and the common, between the unclean and the clean, and so you can teach the Israelites all the decrees the LORD has given them through Moses" (Lev 10:10–11). Drinking clouds judgement. And being a priest was all about judging between the holy and the common, the clean and the unclean; it was about teaching God's will to the people. If you couldn't stay sober, you couldn't do your job.

But while Israel had a priesthood, Israel as a whole was called to *be* a priesthood. After the exodus from Egypt, they were told: "Although the whole earth is mine, you will be for me a kingdom of priests and a holy nation" (Exod 19:5–6). The priests, then, were a kind of distilled version of Israel. Their job was to keep the holy nation holy, so that the nation in turn could fulfil its priestly vocation to all the nations of the earth.

Yet there is a sense in which this notion of 'priesthood', broadly understood, goes back even further. In a way, Adam was a priest and Eden was a priestly garden—a holy space. The original job of humanity was to be a blessing to the world from the garden—to move, in other words, from being blessed by God's presence to blessing the world with his presence.

But after the fall, Adam and Eve are cast out of that garden. The tabernacle was a new Eden, a place where God could dwell with humanity. The fall complicated things. Now it's only the high priest, and only once a year, who goes into the presence of God. And the priest needed to re-learn what Adam was learning: judgement. Just as Adam was called to name (that is, to distinguish between) the animals, so too the priests are called to judgement: to discern and distinguish between the sacred and profane, the holy and the unholy, the clean and the unclean.

All of this is key background to the passage in Leviticus which is central to the debate about worship. It is the story of Nadab and Abihu in Leviticus 10.

"Unauthorized fire" and proper worship

> Aaron's sons Nadab and Abihu took their censers, put fire in them and added incense; and they offered unauthorized fire before the LORD, contrary to his command. So fire came out from the presence of the LORD and consumed them, and they died before the LORD. Moses then said to Aaron, "This is what the LORD spoke of when he said:
>
> "'Among those who approach me
> I will be proved holy;
> in the sight of all the people
> I will be honoured.'"
>
> Aaron remained silent. (Lev 10:1–3)

On first reading, the incident looks like a slam dunk for the regulative principle. What do Nadab and Abihu do wrong? Though they are supposed to be serving the Lord (and the people of Israel) as priests (Exod 28:1), they bring "unauthorized fire" before the Lord, "contrary to his command". They introduce an element into corporate worship not expressly commanded by God. They fail to distinguish the holy. They innovate in worship. And they are judged for it. Severely.

So, has Leviticus settled the matter for us?

My answer, for what it's worth, is yes, no, and sort of.

At some level, the regulative principle must be correct. How could it not be? God chooses how God is worshipped. Worship is not self-actualization. Worship is not self-expression. The moment we say, "The way I like to worship is ..." we've already given the game away. Only God gets to decide how God is worshipped. This must apply to the New Testament too. Can we believe that post-Jesus, God has become disinterested in how people worship him? Surely not!

But here's the twist: in the New Testament, the regulative principle is fulfilled *in Jesus*, not by the church. A church is not the tabernacle, a pastor is not a priest, and the Lord's Supper is not a sacrifice of atonement. These are all things that Jesus fulfilled.

The Gospel of John tells us that Jesus *tabernacled* with us: "The Word became flesh and made his dwelling among us" (John 1:14). Jesus referred to his own body as the temple when he said, "Destroy this temple, and I will raise it again in three days" (John 2:19). Jesus told the Samaritan woman at the well that "a time is coming and has now come when the true worshipers will worship the Father in the Spirit and in truth, for they are the kind of worshipers the Father seeks" (John 4:23). In Hebrews 8, Jesus is literally our 'worship leader'—the one who "serves in the sanctuary, the true tabernacle set up by the Lord" (8:2). Through him we have come to the "joyful assembly" (Heb 12:22).

You see, in the new covenant, God hasn't become more permissive in his worship; he has told us *exactly* how we are to worship him: through Jesus, in the Spirit, and in truth. The regulative principle of the Old Testament stands. Yet it is applied, in the first place, not to what we do in church, but to what we do through Jesus.

In light of the cross, the New Testament teaches that our whole lives are to be lived as worship before God. "I urge you, brothers and sisters, in view of God's mercy, to offer your bodies as a living sacrifice, holy and pleasing to God—this is your true and proper worship" (Rom 12:1). What is proper worship? For us to give our whole selves to him. We're called to be the whole burnt offering to which the offerings of the Old Testament pointed. God gave up his Son for us; we give ourselves to him. That's the worship God requires.

Discerning the holy and the common

The basic principle of Old Testament worship was to discern between the holy and the common. But Leviticus isn't the only place where people die in judgement during corporate worship. It also happens in Corinth, at the Lord's table. Why? What holy thing have they profaned? It's not the bread and the wine. It's the people.

> For those who eat and drink without discerning the body of Christ eat and drink judgement on themselves. That is why many among you are weak and sick, and a number of you have fallen asleep. (1 Cor 11:29–30)

The Corinthians are in trouble because they have failed to discern the body of Christ in the people with whom they were sharing the supper. Some were getting drunk and gorging themselves; others were going hungry. And by doing this, they were failing to treat their brothers and sisters in Christ as holy. Paul instructed them: wait for your brother and sister. Treat them as holy. Discern in them the body of Christ. This is the priestly task of discernment to which all of us are now called.

Years ago, I was a student minister in a church in the inner west of Sydney. It was a wonderful church with a rich variety of members, including several who came from the local men's shelter. One of them, Russell, was non-verbal, profoundly disturbed and smelled as if he went a long time between showers. But he was always there.

I would often kneel next to Russell at the communion rail to receive the bread and the wine. His smell was powerful. His slurping from the common cup was confronting. His mumbling was distracting. What was my job in that moment? To block Russell out of my mind and focus on the holiness of the bread and the wine? To gently warn him that the wine he was spilling down the front of his shirt was holy and that he really ought not be mumbling and distracting the other worshippers? No! My sacred duty in that moment was to see Russell, to rejoice in the fact that I got to share bread and wine with him! It was to treat Russell according to what he really was—a fellow member of the body of Christ, and therefore holy. Through the death of Jesus for him, he was washed, sanctified and justified.

He was holy. My job was to discern the reality that Jesus had already brought about in Russell by his death.

God's fire has not gone out in Jesus. The book of Hebrews tells us that "our 'God is a consuming fire'" (Heb 12:29; see Deut 4:24). The Lord is white hot with holiness. And he fiercely protects his holy things: holy things like Russell, holy things like all those who have been made clean by the blood of Jesus.

That's why we should approach God with reverence and awe. This is why we move towards him in all-of-life worship—not because the fire of his holiness has gone out, but because we have been made holy in Jesus.

Chapter 13

THE COMMUNITY OF THE CROSS

Ambition and resignation

The crucifixion of Jesus was an event in time and space. If you had been there, you could have taken a photograph of it. But today, the cross tends to exist as an idea in our minds. Think of the matters we've already discussed in this book: forgiveness of sins, hope, communion with God, reconciliation, and so on. All these may be real to the person who believes them, but they exist in minds, not things. We believe we have been forgiven, but no X-ray, MRI or blood test will reveal that state to another.

But there *is* something the cross does in our world that happens in time and space, with bodies—an event you could photograph. And that's church. According to the Bible, the cross makes church possible. And the cross gives church a specific character.

What should we expect of church? It is possible to expect too much or to expect too little.

In his book on Christian community, Dietrich Bonhoeffer puts the threat of unrealistic ambition in dramatic terms:

> God hates visionary dreaming; it makes the dreamer proud and pretentious. The man who fashions a visionary ideal of community demands that it be realized by God, by others, and by himself. He enters the community of Christians with his demands, sets up his own law, and judges the brethren and God himself accordingly. He stands adamant, a living reproach to all others in the circle of brethren. He acts as if he is the creator of the Christian community, as if his dream binds men together. When things do not go his way, he calls the effort a failure. When his ideal picture is destroyed, he sees the community going to smash. So he becomes, first the accuser of his brethren, then an accuser of God and finally the despairing accuser of himself.[37]

It's worth knowing that Bonhoeffer wrote this having founded an illegal Christian community under the Nazi regime precisely because he believed in the power and centrality of community in the Christian life. He literally risked (and later lost) his life for the sake of forming

37 D Bonhoeffer, *Life Together* (JW Doberstein trans), 5th edn, SCM Press, 1949, p 16.

deep Christian community. What he was against was an *idealized* community: the community of our imaginations rather than the actual communities into which God places us.

But the other risk is that we expect too little. The New Testament envisages us loving one another, confessing our sins to one another, serving one another, bearing with one another, encouraging one another, teaching one another. Church communities that are less than this aren't 'realistic' or 'the best we can hope for this side of heaven'. They are disobedient.

How can we build, and be part of, the right sort of community? Or, to focus our question a little more precisely, how does the cross of Jesus help us to build the right sort of community?

Freedom from and freedom for: three requirements

The cross sets us free. It sets us free from the power and penalty of sin. It sets us free from the powers and principalities. It sets us free from the coming judgement of God for sin. But what does it set us free *for*? The answer is love. We are set free *from* sin so that we can be freed for love. Freed to "serve one another humbly in love" (Gal 5:13). That life was not possible under the reign of sin. Now it is.

But what does it look like? I've rarely met anyone who is, in principle, anti-love. Most people are pro-love.

Most of us think the more love, the better. But how would you know if you were genuinely living a life of Spirit-empowered love? What would a community look like of which it could be said: "They love each other"? It would be a community in which observers see, in our love for one another, that we are indeed the disciples of Jesus (John 13:34–35). From there, we can track with Galatians 6:1–5 for a moment and prise out three fairly specific answers—answers that are stretching, realistic and cross-shaped.

> Brothers and sisters, if someone is caught in a sin, you who live by the Spirit should restore that person gently. But watch yourselves, or you also may be tempted. Carry each other's burdens, and in this way you will fulfill the law of Christ. If anyone thinks they are something when they are not, they deceive themselves. Each one should test their own actions. Then they can take pride in themselves alone, without comparing themselves to someone else, for each one should carry their own load. (Gal 6:1–5)

1. We will care enough to call out sin in each other's lives

According to Paul, being part of God's family means caring for and taking some measure of responsibility for the other members of the family: "if someone is caught in a sin, you who live by the Spirit should restore that person gently" (v 1). I don't think this means we are supposed to call each other out every time we sin. Sadly, sin is a regular ongoing part of the Christian life, needing daily confession to God. Sometimes, however, Christians are "caught in a sin". Christ's cross has set us free, but we find ourselves again enslaved. Trapped. Caught. What does love look like then?

Love swings into action. We should seek the restoration of the brother or sister who is "caught in a sin". But notice the qualifications: we must do this "gently", and it must be done by someone who is walking "by the Spirit". These are almost always costly interventions. They entail time, grace, emotional energy and spiritual wisdom. But to not act, to not seek the restoration of the other, is to live in ongoing contradiction to the freedom won by the death of Jesus.

The gentleness also speaks to our relationship with each other. Jesus is our Lord and Master. Our sister or brother answers not to us, but to him. Christian community has a crisp, clear org-chart. The line of command goes from Jesus to his servants. We may urge, encourage, rebuke and correct each other. But in the end, "who are you to judge someone else's servant" (Rom 14:4)? Such interventions are both necessary and delicate: necessary, because it's the way of love; delicate, because we approach each other as fellow servants, not commanding officers.

2. We will carry each other's burdens

Most ministers remember their first funeral. It's a bit nerve-wracking. And it's something you want to get right. Mine was for a woman who called our church back in the days of landlines. I picked up the call. She asked for a funeral for her father, and I said we could probably do that. And the senior pastor said I should probably do it. So I did.

On the day of the funeral, I arrived very early at the chapel. I went over my service, practising parts where I might have stumbled. I made sure the music was set up, the chapel seating was right and the lights were on. I met the woman by prior arrangement at the cemetery gate and walked with her back to the chapel, her father's coffin following slowly in the hearse behind us. She took her seat. I went up to the lectern to begin the service. I turned to the congregation to see there were only three people in the room. And only two of us were alive.

I've never forgotten it. Didn't this woman have a single other person in her life to be with her as she buried her dad? Wasn't there someone—a work colleague, a neighbour, a relative, a friend—who could have said, "No-one should bury their father alone—I'll be there with you and help you carry that burden"? In the family of God, this would not merely be sad. It would be a dereliction of duty. Don't leave your brother or sister alone in their hour of need. Carry each other's burdens.

3. We will carry our own load

Hot on the heels of his call to bear one another's burdens, Paul says that "each one should carry their own load" (Gal 6:5). The cross-shaped community is not a place to only ever sit around waiting for someone to help. As far as we are able, we should "carry our own load". God has given us our natural families and assigned specific load-bearing roles there (1 Tim 5:8). And the church is made up of Spirit-filled but finite and fragile human creatures. We should bear our own burdens as we are able so that the community can steward its resources toward those who need the most help.

But it is still an odd and, on the face of it, contradictory pair of injunctions: "Bear one another's burdens" and "carry your own load". How does it work in practice?

In the context, I think it has to do with a realistic assessment of what we might call weight-bearing capacity. Paul warns here against the great joy-robber of the Christian life: comparing ourselves with others (v 4). Almost nothing else is better calculated to steal our hard-won joy in Jesus.

Consider an example: at church, we want everyone to be actively on the lookout for welcoming newcomers each week. That's an everyone job. But the ability of a mother who is also keeping an eye on three children under five to welcome all the new people is very different from that of the empty nester, or the young single, or the parent of older children. For that mother to compare herself to others in that context is no help to anyone, least of all her.

Moreover, as finite and fallen human beings, our weight-bearing capacity is necessarily limited. We are not called to bear burdens *for* people; but we are called to bear burdens *with* people. We can't be what only God can be to another person. We cannot be another person's source of significance and security. Only God can do that. We serve one another well when we can freely and frankly say to each other, "I can't be the solution to your loneliness. I can't fix your marriage. I can't magic away your mental health challenges." We can't say to each other "let me carry that for you". But we can say "can I bear some of that with you?"

I can't be your psychiatrist. But I could drive you to the appointment. I could pray for you while you're there. I could check in a week later to see how it went.

The church can't be the total replacement for your biological family. If you've come from a very broken or dysfunctional family, a church family—no matter how healthy—won't put a lid on that pain. But we can be your in-Christ family. Your brothers and sisters in the family of God, who can walk with you in that.

And we probably can't pay your mortgage. But there may be someone at church who, as they say, "knows a guy". There's probably someone—or at least someone who knows someone, who's really good at financial planning. Someone who would help you reset your mortgage at more favourable settings. Who could help you with saving. Maybe arrange a week of groceries. And so on.

The role of the church

That might all sound a bit modest. That's okay. But through these modest means, God's ambitions for the church are sky high. Through the church, God means to defeat and humiliate the powers of darkness by pulling off a degree-of-difficulty manoeuvre so impressive that even his enemies have to say (albeit reluctantly), "Wow!" That manoeuvre is to bring together Jew and Gentile, slave and free, male and female, and out of them create one new humanity which has been brought together "by the blood of Christ" (Eph 2:13; see vv 11–22). The cross has smashed down the dividing wall of hostility (v 16). Now we get to work out what it looks like to live with smashed walls in the realities of everyday church life.

For first-century Gentiles, this meant yielding to Jewish sensitivities that they found strange and perplexing: food laws, sabbath-keeping, and so on. Paul firmly believed that these obligations were no longer part of the new covenant in Christ. But it's possible to be right and a jerk at the same time: "Accept the one whose faith is weak, without quarrelling over disputable matters" (Rom 14:1). This involves letting a bunch of stuff go through to the keeper.[38] Often, it means setting aside your rights for the sake of the weaker brother. This is the logic of the cross. Christ, equal with God, made himself nothing in order to serve us (Phil 2:6–8). Because of the cross, greatness is service (Mark 10:43–45). What is the cross if not the strong laying aside rights for the sake of the weak?

For Jewish believers, the way of the cross was also costly. It meant setting aside Jewish privilege in order to welcome a bunch of ratbag younger siblings into the

38 Excuse the cricket analogy if you're not from a cricket-playing nation. If you Google it now, you can use it next time you're speaking to someone from Australia, England or India. You're welcome.

family of God. Often, as is the way for firstborns the world over, this meant accepting the low-key annoyance of watching younger siblings do what younger siblings do—getting away with stuff, forgetting to clean up after themselves, and generally interrupting the good thing the family had going when it was just the parents and the first kid. Like the older son in the story of the prodigal son, God's older son (Israel) had the challenge of saying to the younger son (us Gentiles): "Welcome! All that our Father has is yours too!"

The obligation of the strong

Through the cross, our fundamental attitude to the other believer is that "God has accepted them" (Rom 14:3). Their acceptability or otherwise is not our call to make. That ruling is beyond our pay grade. And because of the cross, our Lord and Judge has found in their favour (see Rom 3:24–26, 8:31–34).

This burden falls in particular on The Strong. Both parties, of course, need to yield to each other. The weaker brother or sister doesn't somehow get veto powers over the life of the church. And when scruples become salvation mandates that undermine justification by faith alone (I'm looking at you, the church in Galatia!), all bets are off. But in peaceable times, when backgrounds, upbringing, culture and personality shape us differently on these matters, it's The Strong, *even though they are right*, who are called on to put aside their rights for the sake of The Weak. Why? Because that's the way of the cross:

> We who are strong ought to bear with the failings of the weak and not to please ourselves. Each of us should please our neighbours for their good, to build them up. For even Christ did not please himself but, as it is written: "The insults of those who insult you have fallen on me." (Rom 15:1–3)

Jesus was the Strong One. God the Son, the second person of the Trinity, the one to whom God the Father promised the nations, the heir of Israel's throne, the Lord and Saviour. Jesus was free. He had rights. He had power. He had freedom.

What did he do with it all? He laid it down.

What do you see in the cross? Radical freedom. The sort of freedom that voluntarily lays down rights for the sake of others.

Living in the freedom of the cross

In the 1990s, some Christians took to wearing wristbands with the inscription 'WWJD?'—What Would Jesus Do? It was all a bit kitsch.

But it is a thing. The New Testament does indeed encourage the followers of Jesus to ask the question 'What Would Jesus Do?' But the answer is always the same. The focus is always on a very specific aspect of Jesus' ministry. What would Jesus do? He'd lay down his rights for the sake of the salvation of others. That's what Jesus would do. That's what Jesus *did*.[39]

Christian community is cross-shaped. It is cross-shaped in this very specific manner, whereby The Strong are quietly, repeatedly and consciously looking at their rights and saying, "I'm not going to insist on this. I'm putting my rights aside for the sake of the other."

I recently found myself chatting with a couple after church. They told me they were off on a holiday with some other church couples in the wine region of the southwest of Western Australia. They decided not to take alcohol or visit the vineyards because one of the group's members has recently confessed to a problem with drinking. On Friday nights near our church, a dozen young people in their 20s run a youth program in a school basketball court. Most of them have just come off a busy week at work and could probably think of more relaxing ways to start the weekend. Not long ago I saw Trevor, a well-known surgeon who attends our church, having lunch with a homeless man who has sometimes dropped by on Sundays to see what happens in our services, and to ask for money.

What do those couples, those young people and Trevor all have in common? They are all, in their own ways, examples of people setting aside their rights for the sake of others. Those couples didn't have to have an alcohol-free holiday. Biblically, they were free. But they set aside their rights for the sake of the weaker brother.

39 Maybe WDJD didn't do as well in focus groups?

Running a Friday night youth program isn't a condition of salvation. Any one of those people could say that their Friday nights are for socializing or recovering from a hard week at work. Trevor could have guarded his diary for 'more important' appointments.

These are all, in their own ways, the ripples of the splash left by the cross. They're not generic examples of people being nice; they're specific instances of people looking at something that's well within their rights to insist on and saying, "Nah, I can put that aside for the sake of someone for whom Christ died".

We know a guy

There are some burdens only God can carry. There are some burdens that I cannot and should not put on the community. Christian communities can be great for finding a plumber, a psychologist or a builder. The "I-know-a-guy" culture of churches is a terrific thing. But some needs can't be shared, delegated or subcontracted. The weight of the guilt of my sins, for example—neither you nor the community of the church are meant to carry that burden.

Church can do a lot of great things. But it can't take your sins for you. Your good works can't. Your resolve to do better next time can't. Your diet can't. Your doctor can't.

But I do have some good news for you. We know a guy ...

Appendix

DISCUSSION GUIDE

The questions that follow are designed to help you discuss the content of *Forgiven Forever* with others—your spouse, your friends, or the small group you meet with at church. Use these questions as a way of talking back over the content of each chapter and encouraging one another to put God's word into practice. Feel free to pick and choose your way through the questions, depending on how much time you have available.

Chapter 1: The Jesus meal

1. What are the similarities between Old Testament Israel's situation at the time of the first Passover and the people of God's situation in Jesus' day? What are the differences?
2. How does this understanding of a covenant help you to understand the importance and significance of Jesus' death?

3. In what ways is the 'two-act' version of the gospel deficient? How might the 'four-act' version of the gospel change your Christian life for the better?

A prayer

Gracious heavenly Father, we thank you that Jesus' body was given for us. We praise you that his blood was poured out for us and for many for the forgiveness of sins. Thank you that his death has dealt the decisive blow against the world, the flesh and the devil. Enable us to put off our sin and to live new lives as we await your Son from heaven. In Jesus' name, amen.

Chapter 2: The garden of tears

1. In what ways might the scene in the garden of Gethsemane be seen as a 'problem passage'? How has this chapter helped to solve those problems for you?
2. Jesus prays, "My Father, if it is possible, may this cup be taken from me" (Matt 26:39). Yet his Father still sends him to the cross. What does God's answer to Jesus' prayer tell you about any attempt to relate to God that ignores or relativizes the cross?
3. The garden shows "God with us". What does this mean to you?
4. The garden shows "God instead of us". What does this mean to you?

A prayer

Our Father, we thank you for this glimpse into the heart of your relationship with your beloved Son. Thank you that you offered him for us and instead of us. Lord Jesus, thank you for your obedience to your Father's plan, even to the point of death. Thank you that you drank the cup of God's wrath for us. Amen.

Chapter 3: The song of the cross

1. The Gospel writers offer "simple and sparse" descriptions of the crucifixion. Why is this significant?
2. Take the time to read through Psalm 22. In what ways is it "the song of a believer, not a sceptic"?
3. The cross (along with Psalm 22) establishes the pattern of "first suffering, then glory". How do you feel about this path of discipleship? Where is it playing out in your life?

A prayer

Loving Father, thank you that you were willing to forsake your Son to death so that we might be saved. Thank you that Jesus endured the cross, scorning its shame. Thank you that you rescued him from the grave and that he now leads us in declaring your praises. Equip us to follow faithfully the path of suffering that our Saviour trod, so that we might one day share in his glory. In Jesus' name, amen.

Chapter 4: The sacrificial system for dummies

1. How does the sacrificial system help us to appreciate the "vile" and "disgusting" nature of sin?
2. God is everywhere, and he does not live in temples built by human hands—yet he was with Israel in a special way. How does the Bible address this tension?
3. Can we choose to worship God in our own way? How does the sacrificial system speak to this question?
4. How is the Old Testament sacrificial system relevant today? How might it be part of your efforts to share the gospel with your non-Christian friends?

A prayer

Almighty God, we praise you that you are holy, and that the whole earth is full of your glory. Yet we thank you that you chose to dwell with your people in the Old Testament. Thank you for the provision of the sacrificial system. Help us to see our sin as vile and disgusting. Enable us to see and understand your holiness, so that we may be holy. In Jesus' name, amen.

Chapter 5: Jesus our Great High Priest

1. Have you ever been "confused, perplexed or disappointed by the continuing presence of sin in your life"? How has this chapter helped you in those struggles?
2. Jesus "knows temptation more intimately than we do—not despite the fact that he never gave in to it, but *because* he never gave into it". How does this help you understand the nature of temptation? How does it help you understand Jesus?
3. Have you ever fallen into the trap of trying to "get things in order" before coming to Jesus? How can the truths covered in this chapter help you to avoid this trap?

A prayer

Gracious Father, thank you for Jesus Christ—the Great High Priest that we need. Lord Jesus, we praise you that you have been tempted in every way, yet you did not sin. Thank you that you can help us when we are tempted and that you live to intercede for us. Lord, when we are tempted, help us. Come to our aid. Lead us not into temptation, and deliver us from the evil one. We need you, and we trust you. Amen.

Chapter 6: Jesus our sacrifice

1. How is “the infinite worth” of Jesus’ person central to the cross?
2. In what ways do you need to heed the warning associated with Christ’s sacrifice? What difference might this make in your life?
3. In what ways do you need to remember the assurance associated with Christ’s sacrifice? What difference might this make in your life?

A prayer

Heavenly Father, thank you that your perfect Son died as the perfect sacrifice for our sins. Thank you that he threw open the doors to your mercy. Enable us to heed the warnings from your word so that we will never walk away from your provision of salvation. Help us also to remember the assurance offered by your word and to hold fast to your promise of forgiveness. We praise you that we can have confidence to enter the Most Holy Place by the blood of Jesus, shed for us. In Jesus’ name, amen.

Chapter 7: In our place condemned he stood: How the cross deals with guilt

1. Have you been exposed to the controversy around ‘penal substitutionary atonement’ before reading this chapter? What was your initial response to the controversy?
2. Do you struggle with the ideas that our sin deserves a penalty and that “the wages of sin is death” (Rom 6:23)? Why or why not? How did this chapter help you to understand these ideas?
3. According to the Bible, what is good about guilt? What is bad about guilt?

4. Look back over the three key objections stated as questions. Having read through the chapter, how would you answer each of these objections in your own words? How would you answer them for a Christian friend struggling with the objections?

A prayer

Gracious God, we praise you that you are both perfectly holy and perfectly merciful. Thank you that you brought your love and justice together at the cross. We praise you that, though we have sinned and fallen short of your glory, there is now no condemnation or guilt for those who are in Christ. Enable us to trust the finished work of your Son and to trust your gracious, life-giving promises. In Jesus' name, amen.

Chapter 8: Silencing Grandma: How the cross deals with our shame

1. According to the Bible, what is good about shame? What is bad about shame?
2. In what ways was Jesus shamed in his life and in his death?
3. Have you experienced the "negative social consequences" of being a Christian? If so, "Jesus has gone there too"—how does this shape your perspective on your experiences (or on possible future experiences)?
4. Jesus said, "If anyone is ashamed of me and my words in this adulterous and sinful generation, the Son of Man will be ashamed of them when he comes in his Father's glory with the holy angels" (Mark 8:38). In the context of everything this chapter says about the cross and shame, what is your response to these words from Jesus?

A prayer

Dear Father, thank you that Jesus is the pioneer and perfecter of our faith. Thank you that he went from honour to shame so that we can go from shame to honour. Equip us now to take up our cross and follow him. Strengthen us to never be ashamed of Jesus, so that he will not be ashamed of us when he comes in your glory. Help us to consider him, so that we will not grow weary or lose heart. We ask this through Jesus our Lord, amen.

Chapter 9: Power and leadership: How the cross makes leaders servants and servants leaders

1. How is Jesus' way different from the Jewish and Greek leadership ideals that were affecting the Corinthian church?
2. Have you witnessed the difference between Christian leaders who get 'servant leadership' right and Christian leaders who fail to be 'servant leaders'? How do these differences affect the lives of the people they lead?
3. "No more boasting about human leaders!" (1 Cor 3:21). Have you ever been tempted to boast in a human leader? How does the cross address this temptation?

A prayer

Dear heavenly Father, thank you that the message of the cross is "the power of God". Please reshape all our thoughts about leadership and service in light of the cross. When we lead, enable us to be godly servant leaders who never lord it over others, but instead make ourselves the slave of all. When we follow, give us godly leaders, and help us to honour them without boasting about them. May we boast only in you, Lord. In Jesus' name, amen.

Chapter 10: A user's guide to the Lord's Supper

1. At the Last Supper, Jesus took the cup and said, "This cup is the new covenant in my blood, which is poured out for you" (Luke 22:20). Why is this proclamation of "the new covenant" so significant?
2. "The cross binds us simultaneously to Christ and to each other". How does this biblical truth shape the way you think about the Lord's Supper?
3. In what sense can we rightly say that the cross is 'political'? What does this have to do with the Lord's Supper in our churches?

A prayer

Loving heavenly Father, thank you that we were baptized into Christ's death—that we died with him and in him. Thank you that Christ's blood was poured out for us to establish the new covenant, and thank you for the covenant renewal ceremony of the Lord's Supper. Whenever and wherever we share the Supper, enable us to proclaim the power and glory of the cross to each other and to the world. Through Jesus, our Lord and Saviour, amen.

Chapter 11: How to use the cross in the event of a zombie apocalypse

1. Who is our enemy? What different answers does the Bible give?
2. "Evil at its most evil accidentally undoes evil". How does this explain what happened at the cross?
3. Jesus "disarmed the powers and authorities" at the cross (Col 2:15). What will it look like for you to live your life in the wake of that victory?

A prayer

Almighty God, you alone are sovereign over the whole universe. You rule our world, and you rule the unseen world of the "powers and authorities". We praise you that, in his death, Jesus has disarmed and defeated every force that is opposed to you. Thank you that our sin and guilt have been taken away, so that the Accuser now has no power over us. Help us to live our lives in the wake of this victory, to your glory. Through Jesus Christ our Lord, amen.

Chapter 12: The cross and what we do in church

1. Which principle best fits your experience(s) of church: the 'regulative principle', or the 'normative principle'? Which principle do you think is the more biblical?
2. What is the worship that God requires? How is this worship related to the death of Jesus?
3. Is there anything practical or specific you can do to ensure that you are "discerning the body of Christ" (1Cor 11:29) in others when you next share the Lord's Supper?

A prayer

Loving heavenly Father, thank you for Jesus, our worship leader, who has brought us to the joyful assembly. Father, we long to give you your true and proper worship. Enable us, in view of your mercy, to offer our bodies as living sacrifices, holy and pleasing to you. May our churches be places where we offer the worship that you require and where we discern in each other the body of Christ. In Jesus' name, amen.

Chapter 13: The community of the cross

1. Biblically, what are we freed *from*? What are we freed *for*?
2. Pick one of the three points drawn from Galatians 6 and think of a practical application that is relevant for you now. What will you do to put this into practice?
3. "Because of the cross, greatness is service". Where are you serving? How is your service shaped by the cross?
4. "We who are strong ought to bear with the failings of the weak and not to please ourselves ... For even Christ did not please himself" (Rom 15:1, 3). How can you use your freedom, won for you at the cross, for the sake of others?

A prayer

Gracious God, thank you for the cross—foolishness to those who are perishing, but the power of God to those of us who are being saved. Enable us to deny ourselves, take up our cross, and follow the Lord Jesus. Make us willing and able to lose our lives for Jesus and his gospel. Give us opportunities to share the life-changing news of the cross with others who are ready to listen. And lead us to the foot of the cross every day. We pray these things for Jesus' sake and for his glory. Amen.

Acknowledgements

I would like to thank Andrew Moody at The Gospel Coalition Australia for allowing some of this material to get its first run at the website. Thanks also to Charlotte Butler, Mikey Lynch, David Mitchell, Tamara Robson and Bethany Smith for reading an earlier version of the book and making many valuable suggestions for improvement. And thank you to my editor, Geoff Robson, for his constant encouragement and patience.

Feedback on this resource

We really appreciate getting feedback about our resources—not just suggestions for how to improve them, but also positive feedback and ways they can be used. We especially love to hear that the resources may have helped someone in their Christian growth.

You can send feedback to us via the 'Feedback' menu in our online store, or write to us at info@matthiasmedia.com.au.

matthiasmedia

Matthias Media is an evangelical publishing ministry that seeks to persuade all Christians of the truth of God's purposes in Jesus Christ as revealed in the Bible, and equip them with high-quality resources, so that by the work of the Holy Spirit they will:

- abandon their lives to the honour and service of Christ in daily holiness and decision-making
- pray constantly in Christ's name for the fruitfulness and growth of his gospel
- speak the Bible's life-changing word whenever and however they can—in the home, in the world and in the fellowship of his people.

Our wide range of resources includes Bible studies, books, training courses, tracts and children's material. To find out more, and to access samples and free downloads, visit our website:

www.matthiasmedia.com

How to buy our resources

1. Direct from us over the internet:
   - in the US: www.matthiasmedia.com
   - in Australia: www.matthiasmedia.com.au
2. Direct from us by phone: please visit our website for current phone contact information.
3. Through a range of outlets in various parts of the world. Visit **www.matthiasmedia.com/contact** for details about recommended retailers in your part of the world.
4. Trade enquiries can be addressed to:
   - in the US and Canada: sales@matthiasmedia.com
   - in Australia and the rest of the world: sales@matthiasmedia.com.au

Register at our website for our **free** regular email update to receive information about the latest new resources, **exclusive special offers**, and free articles to help you grow in your Christian life and ministry.

Also by Rory Shiner

One Forever

When the New Testament describes what it means to be a Christian, it uses a phrase that is everywhere in Paul's letters but almost nowhere in our churches. Overwhelmingly, when the Bible wants to describe being a Christian, it says that we are "in Christ".

But what does it mean to be in Christ? And how does this important biblical idea help us understand what God has done for us through Jesus and what it means to be a Christian?

This short book by Rory Shiner sparkles with clarity, wit and biblical wisdom on this vital and much-neglected topic.

FOR MORE INFORMATION OR TO ORDER CONTACT:

Matthias Media
Email: sales@matthiasmedia.com.au
www.matthiasmedia.com.au

Matthias Media (USA)
Email: sales@matthiasmedia.com
www.matthiasmedia.com

Also by Rory Shiner

Raised Forever

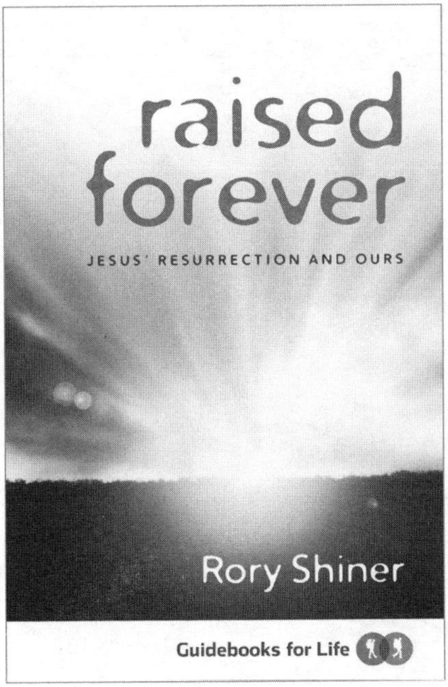

For many Christians, believing that God raised Jesus from death becomes an assumed but unexamined truth, and studying the resurrection is left to those who wish to explore the historical evidence for it. But how exactly do we connect what happened to Jesus 2000 years ago with our lives today?

With his characteristic warmth, wit and wisdom, Rory Shiner delves into the Bible's teaching on this central yet often misunderstood topic, showing how Jesus' resurrection has a profound effect on our past, our present and our future. Surveying the historical evidence for Jesus' resurrection, *Raised Forever* digs beneath the surface to show what the events of the first Easter Sunday reveal about Jesus' identity, as well as the life-changing implications of the early Christian claims about Jesus.

This book will open your eyes to see that the biblical teaching on the resurrection is deeper, richer and more compelling than most of us ever imagined.

FOR MORE INFORMATION OR TO ORDER CONTACT:

Matthias Media
Email: sales@matthiasmedia.com.au
www.matthiasmedia.com.au

Matthias Media (USA)
Email: sales@matthiasmedia.com
www.matthiasmedia.com